D1328317

THE TEACHING OF VALUES AND ETHICS IN SOCIAL WORK EDUCATION

The Teaching of Values and Ethics in Social Work Education

MURIEL W. PUMPHREY

VOLUME XIII

A Project Report of the Curriculum Study
Werner W. Boehm, Director and Coordinator

COUNCIL ON SOCIAL WORK EDUCATION
345 EAST 46TH STREET, NEW YORK 17, N. Y.

Copyright ©, 1959
by the
COUNCIL ON SOCIAL WORK EDUCATION
INCORPORATED
Library of Congress Catalog Number: 59-12424

60
Printed in the United States of America
by H. Wolff Book Manufacturing Co., Inc.

361.301
P98 34

PANEL PARTICIPANTS

The affiliations listed are those of the participants at the time of panel membership.

Chairman

Reverend Vincent de Paul Lee, S.J.
School of Social Service
Fordham University
New York, New York

Herbert Aptekar
Jewish Community Services of Long
*   Island*
Jamaica, New York

Antoinette Cannon
James Weldon Johnson Community
*   Center*
New York, New York

Catherine Casey
Massachusetts Department of Public
*   Health*
Boston, Massachusetts

James R. Dumpson
Department of Welfare
New York, New York

Goldie Basch Faith
School of Social Work
University of Pennsylvania
Philadelphia, Pennsylvania

Arthur Katz
School of Social Work
Adelphi College
Garden City, New York

Hertha Kraus
Graduate Department of Social Work
*   and Social Research*
Bryn Mawr College
Bryn Mawr, Pennsylvania

Verl S. Lewis
School of Social Work
University of Connecticut
Hartford, Connecticut

Gertrude Leyendecker
Community Service Society
New York, New York

Jean M. Maxwell
Graduate School of Public Adminis-
*   tration and Social Service*
New York University
New York, New York

Robert F. Rutherford
School of Social Work
Simmons College
Boston, Massachusetts

Morton Teicher
School of Social Work
Yeshiva University
New York, New York

Caroline F. Ware
School of Social Work
Howard University
Washington, D.C.

44142

Corresponding Members of Panel on Values and Ethics

Richard Guilford
Graduate School of Social Work
University of Nebraska
Lincoln, Nebraska

Louis H. Towley
George Warren Brown School of
  Social Work
Washington University
St. Louis, Missouri

Leon Lucas
School of Social Work
Wayne State University
Detroit, Michigan

Elizabeth Wisner
School of Social Work
Tulane University
New Orleans, Louisiana

Members of Special Panel for Definitions for the Project on Values and Ethics

Chairman

Reverend Vincent de Paul Lee, S.J.
School of Social Service
Fordham University
New York, New York

Horace M. Kallen
New School for Social Research
New York, New York

Reverend Thomas J. Bigham, Jr.
General Theological Seminary
New York, New York

Mordecai Kaplan
Jewish Theological Seminary
New York, New York

Charles Frankel
Columbia University
New York, New York

Robert M. MacIver
Juvenile Delinquency Evaluation
  Project
The City College
New York, New York

Reverend Joseph D. Hassett
School of Education
Fordham University
New York, New York

F. Ernest Johnson
National Council of the Churches of
  Christ in the U.S.A.
New York, New York

Elizabeth Salmon
Department of Philosophy
Fordham University
New York, New York

Project Director

Muriel W. Pumphrey, D.S.W.
Community Service Society
New York, New York

PUBLISHER'S NOTE

Board Policy

This project report of the Curriculum Study is published in accordance with the policy adopted by the Board of Directors of the Council at its meeting on October 9–11, 1958. The policy adopted provides that:

The content of Curriculum Study reports are the responsibility of the Curriculum Study staff;

These reports will be published by the Council as submitted to it by the Study staff and given the widest possible distribution;

The Council, through all possible channels, shall encourage thorough consideration and discussion of the findings and recommendations and their implications for social work education and practice.

The Board decided further that:

Publication and distribution of the Curriculum Study reports does not imply Council acceptance of the findings or recommendations;

Implementation of any of the recommendations of the Study can come only after the field has had full opportunity to consider the reports, the appropriate bodies of the Council have considered and recommended action which would modify or change existing policies and standards.

The Board sincerely hopes that the many challenging questions which the Study presents will be given the mature, deliberate and objective consideration they merit and which characterize the true profession.

The Board wishes to register on behalf of the Council its sincere appreciation to the Study staff whose dedicated service brought the Curriculum Study to a successful conclusion.

The thirteen volumes of the Curriculum Study have been numbered to facilitate reference and identification. The comprehensive report has been numbered Volume I, the report on undergraduate education because of its comprehensive nature has been numbered Volume II. The other volumes have been numbered in alphabetical order by title as follows:

VOL.

I   OBJECTIVES FOR THE SOCIAL WORK CURRICULUM OF THE FUTURE

II   THE PLACE OF THE UNDERGRADUATE CURRICULUM IN SOCIAL WORK EDUCATION

III   THE ADMINISTRATION METHOD IN SOCIAL WORK EDUCATION

IV   THE COMMUNITY ORGANIZATION METHOD IN SOCIAL WORK EDUCATION

V   EDUCATION FOR SOCIAL WORKERS IN THE CORRECTIONAL FIELD

VI   AN ORIENTATION TO KNOWLEDGE OF HUMAN GROWTH AND BEHAVIOR IN SOCIAL WORK EDUCATION

VII EDUCATION FOR SOCIAL WORKERS IN THE PUBLIC SOCIAL SERVICES

VIII EDUCATION FOR SOCIAL WORKERS IN THE REHABILITATION OF THE HANDICAPPED

IX   THE RESEARCH METHOD IN SOCIAL WORK EDUCATION

X   THE SOCIAL CASEWORK METHOD IN SOCIAL WORK EDUCATION

XI   THE SOCIAL GROUP WORK METHOD IN SOCIAL WORK EDUCATION

XII SOCIAL WELFARE POLICY AND SERVICES IN SOCIAL WORK EDUCATION

XIII THE TEACHING OF VALUES AND ETHICS IN SOCIAL WORK EDUCATION

Acknowledgments

The Board is pleased to make public acknowledgment of its appreciation to the following foundations and organizations whose grants made possible the financing of this Curriculum Study:

FIELD FOUNDATION

ITTLESON FAMILY FOUNDATION

NATIONAL INSTITUTE OF MENTAL HEALTH, DEPARTMENT OF HEALTH, EDUCATION, AND WELFARE

NATIONAL TUBERCULOSIS ASSOCIATION

NEW YORK FUND FOR CHILDREN

OFFICE OF VOCATIONAL REHABILITATION, DEPARTMENT OF HEALTH, EDUCATION, AND WELFARE

ROCKEFELLER BROTHERS FUND

Although all projects of the Curriculum Study were interdependent and each contributed to the others and to the comprehensive report—and the staff worked as a team under one director—certain grants were more particularly earmarked for designated projects. Accordingly, acknowledgment is made of this circumstance in the appropriate volumes.

In addition to grants from these organizations, the Council on Social Work Education made substantial contributions from its own funds.

—Ernest F. Witte

New York, New York   *Executive Director*

May, 1959   *Council on Social Work Education*

Preface

This comprehensive three-year study of curriculum in the education of social workers has been completed under the auspices of the Council on Social Work Education. It has comprised twelve separate projects, one of which is reported in the following pages.

The twelve individual project reports are published separately by the Council to meet the needs of social work educators and practitioners whose interest is especially concentrated in the subject matter of one or more of the projects. No single report, however, can be understood in its proper relation to the whole study without reference to the comprehensive report, *Objectives for the Social Work Curriculum of the Future,* in which the findings and recommendations of the total study are presented. The various project directors worked together as a staff under the over-all guidance of Dr. Werner W. Boehm, Director and Coordinator of the Curriculum Study. Their goal was not only to develop desirable educational objectives for each project's particular area of the curriculum or suggested by particular considerations of practice, but, in addition, to do so in a way that would merge them all into a total educational experience.

Each project was designed to fit into a master plan for the study of the total curriculum. The findings and recommendations of each are relevant to those of the whole Study and have in turn been influenced by all other projects. To be understood, each report must therefore be considered in relation to the comprehensive report, which it supplements by supplying details for the particular area of the social work curriculum.

WHY THE STUDY WAS UNDERTAKEN

Many issues facing social work education were identified in the Hollis-Taylor Report of 1951.[1] It confirmed that the great preponderance of persons engaged in social work activities were still without professional education. It raised such questions as:

Does social work have a well-defined and identified function?

Does it possess a systematic body of knowledge, skills and attitudes in the various areas of social work practice?

Is the content of social work education sufficiently well developed so that it can be transmitted, and is it of such caliber that it can be included properly as a professional discipline within a university?

Progress toward answering these questions was made by the adoption of the Council's Curriculum Policy Statement in 1952, but further study was indicated. Social work education had also to face other issues:

How could it meet the greatly increased need for social work personnel?

How best could it train for a professional practice still in the process of rapid change and development? Can it be broad enough in scope to enable social workers to function in fields just emerging as well as those already established? Will breadth of education to encompass all fields of professional practice result in dilution of competence for specific fields?

How could it inculcate qualities of leadership and statesmanship while at the same time training for competence in specific practice?

Should undergraduate education serve primarily as a basis for graduate training or also prepare personnel for certain social work positions?

The Study considered that materials from which answers to all these questions might emerge would be obtained by focusing upon

[1] Ernest V. Hollis and Alice L. Taylor, *Social Work Education in the United States* (New York: Columbia University Press, 1951).

fundamental questions of curriculum planning and not by piece-meal consideration of the specific questions posed. In education for social work as for other professions, the fundamental considerations in curriculum planning apply, as presented succinctly by Dr. Ralph W. Tyler.[2] Paraphrased for purposes of this study they are:

What are the desirable educational objectives for professional education?

What learning experiences should be selected and devised and how organized, to realize these objectives?

What are the effective means of evaluating whether the objectives have been attained?

Without a clear formulation of the objectives of social work education, that is, the knowledge, skills and attitudes students are expected to acquire, it becomes impossible to plan the learning experiences needed or to evaluate their success. Consequently, the Curriculum Study singled out as its major task identification of the desirable objectives of social work education.

Also, in accordance with Dr. Tyler's definition, each project framed its educational objectives in terms of both the *content* to be covered and the kind and quality of *behavior* to be expected from the student in relation to the content. For example, "familiarity" with a certain area of content becomes distinguishable from behaviors involving more complex manipulations or deeper "understanding" of content at other levels of student learning.

HOW THE STUDY WAS CARRIED ON

The individual projects of the study fell into the following major areas:

1. Specific curriculum areas—projects devised to examine the curriculum in the areas identified by the Curriculum Policy Statement of 1952: Human Growth and Behavior, the Social

2 Ralph W. Tyler, *Basic Principles of Curriculum and Instruction* (Chicago: The University of Chicago Press, 1950).

Services, Social Work Methods (casework, group work, community organization, research, administration).

2. Selected fields of practice—projects devised to study elements of practice in rehabilitation, public social services, and corrections.
3. Undergraduate education for social work.
4. Content on social work values and ethics found throughout the curriculum.

Each project was planned to identify educational objectives in existing curricula; to formulate a series of desirable objectives, the desirability of which was determined by judging their importance, consistency and compatibility with a statement of the nature and function of social work; and to review the objectives in the light of educational theory as to the possibility of their being learned in the time and conditions available. Project directors had consultation and assistance from specially selected panels of educators and practitioners in social work and related disciplines.

WHAT THE STUDY HOPES TO ACCOMPLISH

Responsibility for planning and constructing curriculum belongs basically to the social work schools and departments. As a group they have already come far toward definition of common educational goals for the profession and of content all curricula must have to reach such goals. The Curriculum Study is expected to provide guides for the resolution of the major issues and common questions that it is anticipated will arise in the curriculum planning of all member schools and departments of the Council on Social Work Education.

Contents

PANEL PARTICIPANTS V

PUBLISHER'S NOTE vii

PREFACE ix

INTRODUCTION 3

I THE PLACE OF VALUES AND ETHICS IN
PROFESSIONAL EDUCATION 8

In Any Profession 8
Social Work Adaptation of the Service Ideal 11
Issues and Uncertainties 13

II METHODOLOGY AND NATURE OF DATA 22

Scope of Project 22
Working Definitions 23
Sources of Data 26
Process of Data Analysis 34

III THE CHARACTERISTICS OF SOCIAL WORK
VALUES AND ETHICS: HOW THEY OCCUR
IN THE LEARNING PROCESS 37

Semantics 37
Values at Varying Levels of Abstraction 40
The Ethics of the Profession 50
Conclusions 61

IV THE NATURE OF THE LEARNING PROCESS
WITH RESPECT TO VALUES 62

Preparation and Readiness to Learn 62
Stages in Learning 65
Levels of Understanding of Values 70
Variations in Learning Patterns 76

V EDUCATIONAL OBJECTIVES FOR THE
TEACHING OF VALUES AND ETHICS 79

CONCLUSIONS 119

APPENDIX A: SUGGESTED CURRICULUM
ORGANIZATION 124

APPENDIX B: QUESTIONNAIRE TO GRADUATE
SCHOOLS OF SOCIAL WORK 135

APPEDIX C: COMPILATION OF ANSWERS TO
ONE ITEM OF THE QUESTIONNAIRE 138

APPENDIX D: LIST OF WORDS
ENCOUNTERED 141

APPENDIX E: CLASSIFIED BIBLIOGRAPHY 144

SELECTED BIBLIOGRAPHY 147

Introduction

When this part of the Curriculum Study was projected in the fall of 1956, preliminary perusal of class materials, educational committee reports and professional literature indicated that no comprehensive effort to define the exact content of this part of the total learning experience had ever been attempted. This remained true although at the Annual Meeting of the American Association of Schools of Social Work in 1952, discussions of the common skills and understandings in all social work practice had referred frequently to the need for clarifying what should be taught regarding the philosophic base and ethical formulations of the profession.[1]

Neither was there much clear-cut delineation of how social work practitioners utilize such material in their daily tasks which might serve as a guide in planning education for use. Like Mark Twain's classic observation on the status of weather control, many people talked about need for more organized philosophic learning, but few had done anything about it. In contrast to other curriculum areas which had benefited from years of detailed course and sequence formulation, repeated experimentation, and testing in beginning practice, very little previous group thinking or codified and critically appraised educational experience was available for examination. It appeared that educators and the agencies hiring the graduates of our schools had progressed only to the point of thinking that systematic attention should be directed to this area of content.

Because less than one year's work by a part-time project director could be allocated to this project, it was decided in staff consultation that the study could most profitably concentrate on exploration of the factors that might be involved, the issues and alternatives that would have to be taken into account in planning curriculum for

1 American Association of Schools of Social Work, *Towards an Integrated Program of Professional Education for Social Work: Summary and Findings of Four Workshops,* Annual Meeting, American Association of Schools of Social Work, 1952 (New York: AASSW, 1952), Section II, esp. 4, 7.

values and ethics. At the outset, it was seen that opinion leaned to the belief that this kind of learning takes place in the entire school experience. Therefore, in order to have any realistic significance, observations would have to be drawn from all courses; the entire curriculum would have to be reviewed from this particular standpoint. With so scanty a base of possibilities for allocating value content in courses, and the limited time to be donated to it, the project might foreseeably be able to accomplish only a preliminary listing of considerations that would require a later, more intensive approach. Any conclusions derived would of necessity be of a highly tentative descriptive nature, rather than definitive.[2]

Not only was there general vagueness as to the exact kind of value behavior required in social work practice but also there appeared to be a dearth of information in related social science fields which could suggest from previous research how to go about seeking the answers. Studies of the kinds of attitudes held by people abounded, but empirical research on how these attitudes came to be was scarce, and objective studies of how attitudes might purposely be fostered or modified were almost nonexistent. Most statements were based on speculation and hypotheses. Only a few authors seemed to have grappled with the problem of how values can be taught at any level,[3] even fewer had probed into how such learning takes place in adults.[4] Much time was consumed in trying to devise a research approach in this almost totally unchartered

[2] For levels of Research see Marie Jahoda *et al., Research Methods in Social Relations,* Part I (New York: The Dryden Press, 1951), Chapter III. The level of this study roughly corresponds to her description of formulative or exploratory studies, 32–47.
[3] See Classified Bibliography, "How Values Are Learned," Appendix E.
[4] Notable among these are Kurt Lewin, "Conduct, Knowledge, and Acceptance of New Values," in *Resolving Social Conflicts,* ed. by Gertrude W. Lewin (New York: Harper & Bros., 1948), 56–68; Manuel Barkan, and Ross L. Mooney, *Conference on Creativity: A Report to the Rockefeller Foundation* (Columbus: Ohio State University, 1953); Francis Levinson Beatman, "How Do Professional Workers Become Professional?" in *Casework Papers, 1956,* from the National Conference of Social Work (New York: Family Service Association of America, 1956), 27–36; William Clayton Bower, *Moral and Spiritual Values in Education* (Lexington: University of Kentucky Press, 1952); Talcott Parsons, *Religious Perspective of College Teaching in Sociology Social Psychology* (New Haven: Edward W. Hogan Foundation, 1951); Charlotte Towle, *The Learner in Education for the Professions* (Chicago: University of Chicago Press, 1954). The work of the Massachusetts Institute of Technology in the Summer Seminar on Creative Engineering, 1955, and the activities of the Bureau of Educational Research, Ohio University, were the best examples this author located of preliminary thinking in this area as related to professional education.

area. The final research design comprised a number of possible ways of getting at the nature of problems involved on an extensive rather than definitive level.[5] In a very real sense, the entire project has taken on somewhat the character of a preliminary pilot study of possible methodologies, none of which could be tested sufficiently for certain prediction of usefulness.

Following the Tyler approach to curriculum planning which provides the framework of the entire Curriculum Study, the first consideration was to appraise the purpose of value and ethical learning in the total learning experience. To do this, it was necessary to consider the socio-cultural and personality-growth functions of this component in professional life. What uses do persons in any profession make of values and ethics? Chapter I is a brief synthesis of thinking from sociology, anthropology, and "dynamic psychology" about the contribution of philosophic-ethical content to professional development in general, and how it fits into the tradition and the current professional needs of social work in particular.

Chapter II is an appraisal of the various sources of data and methods used to explore the problem, with suggestions for more detailed and definitive explorations in the future.

Chapter III analyzes what little has so far been accumulated as to the content of current social work thinking and practice concerning values and ethics, in an effort to determine what knowledge may have a bearing and what kinds of behaviors are deemed essential to adequate professional functioning at the beginning level of practice.

Chapter IV discusses the learning process with respect to values from the point of view of the learner—what he is like in the beginning with respect to his value and ethical formulations, the kinds of blockings and typical psychological movement he may experience, and some scattered observations of learning experiences which have had demonstrated meaning to students.

In Chapter V an attempt is made to formulate a list of desirable educational objectives which, in the light of professional needs

[5] "Plan for the Study of Values and Ethics in the Social Work Curriculum," (New York: Council on Social Work Education, #7–76–1, January 22, 1957), and "Working Definitions of Terms (New York: Council on Social Work Education, #7–76–2, January 22, 1957, mimeographed).

and student qualities, ought to be kept in mind when learning experiences are designed—objectives which will guide efforts to help the student change from the kind of person he is likely to be in his first semester to the kind of person whose professional behavior will be that expected of a trained social worker. Stated at their highest level of generality these objectives are:

Comprehension of values, disvalues, and ethical judgments as human phenomena-understanding of the philosophic-spiritual component in every life situation.

Appreciation of different value systems, including one's own.

Awareness of typical professional positions with respect to values and ethics.

Ability to interpret social work value positions.

Ability to withstand pressures to change value positions and ethical judgments.

Recognition of classic conflict positions in a social work situation.

Ability to use professional procedures and channels in solving conflicts.

Appreciation of common ultimate goals of many branches of the profession and recognition of unity of purpose in these diverse efforts.

Ability to use one's own value systems in a helping relationship.

Use of common professional goals as motivation for professional creativity.

These objectives have been reviewed by the staff of the Curriculum Study and by an advisory panel of educators and advanced practitioners. The author wishes to acknowledge the great help given by the two panels, and by faculty members in schools throughout the country who generously took time for interviews and to answer questionnaires and letters of inquiry. While the opinions expressed, unless otherwise stated, are the author's own, they have been arrived at or clarified by much group thinking, formal and informal.

The purpose of this project, as the author sees it, will have been accomplished if it should set educators thinking and experimenting further, and especially if it should be quickly outmoded by testing of these educational experiments in the practice of the social workers in whose training they have been applied. If past experience in the process of curriculum formulation is any indication, one would hope that the attention of professional groups in workshops and committee will be directed systematically to the area of values and ethics. The planned teaching of values and ethics is one of the frontiers of social work where much pioneering is needed. This report is not a finished map to guide such pioneers, but perhaps can serve as a crude compass to point some directions along which exploration may be organized.

CHAPTER I

The Place of Values and Ethics in Professional Education

IN ANY PROFESSION

Those who have grappled with the problem of delineating the nature of the concept, "profession," have suggested many different distinguishing traits on which there is little unanimity; but they have been surprisingly consistent in identifying two characteristcs.[1]

First, any profession stands *for* something which it deems highly essential to the common good of society, and which its practitioners firmly believe they have a unique part in providing as a service to the rest of society. However partial the actual fulfillment of this ideal, the ideal is there as a central, indispensable theme in all professional activity. Medicine visualizes a state of increasing longevity and optimum health; law upholds the idea of universal order and justice; education idealizes general possession of and intelligent use of mankind's accumulated experience; the librarian hopes for preservation of and easy accessibility to man's collected learning and creative thought. These values [2] are not unique to the profession concerned—in fact most members of society probably would affirm their desirability in varying degree—but while many other people may contribute to its realization, working toward the

---

[1] *E.g.,* see Robert D. Kohn, "Introductory Remarks," in *The Future of the Professions in America.* Proceedings of the Second Institute on Human Relations of the New York Society for Ethical Culture, n. d.; Lloyd E. Blauch (ed.), *Education for the Professions* (Washington, D.C.: United States Department of Health, Education, and Welfare, 1955), 2, 4; Morris L. Cogan, "Toward a Definition of Profession," *The Harvard Educational Review,* XXIII (Winter, 1953), 33–50, esp. 39, "The evidence examined strongly supports the idea that profession is permeated with positive values" and 46, "The professional is the conservator and representative of value that modern society is seeking to preserve"; Morris L. Cogan, "The Problem of Defining a Profession," 105–111, and Robert MacIver, "The Social Significance of Professional Ethics," 118–124, in "Ethical Standards and Professional Conduct," (a symposium) ed. by Benson Y. Landis, *The Annals of the American Academy of Political and Social Science,* CCVII (January, 1955); Ernest Greenwood, "Attributes of a Profession," *Social Work,* II, 3 (July, 1957), 50–53; Ray Lewis and Angus Maude, *Professional People* (London: Phoenix House, Ltd., 1952), 58–59.

[2] For definition of values see Chapter II, 13.

ideal is regarded as the special province of the profession. The enlargement and continuous redefinition of the meaning of the ideal and of means for its attainment are accepted as the paramount responsibility of every member of the profession. For the professional person, the professional ideal assumes priority for attention among many generally accepted goals for mankind.

Each profession also has idealistic words to describe what it does in its attempt to attain the ideal state to which it looks forward. They often take on mystical or symbolic meaning. Traditionally, the clergyman "saves," the nurse "comforts," the physician "heals," the engineer "designs" and "builds." The social worker has always "helped," and more recently "enables" and "facilitates."

A second professional trait is almost as uniformly noted. The members of a profession formulate a collectively sponsored statement concerning recommended behavior for practitioners, behavior which is deemed most likely to result in achievement of the ideal toward which the profession is focused, and which will preserve and enhance the profession for continued usefulness. The prescriptions vary from highly generalized, platitudinous descriptions to extremely explicit rules and directives, from tentative suggestions to absolute demands backed by legal sanctions; but all attempt to make clear what is acceptable or questionable conduct for practicing professionals and to make explicit the behavior expectations that members of the profession agree it is reasonable to associate with carrying out the role of a recognized member of their service-giving group.

Some sociologists and scholars observing professional characteristics have called attention to dangers in a narrow commitment to professional ideals and ethics.[3] A profession may become ingrown and lose sight of the fact that other professions and all society may be headed toward similar goals. Ethical demands may be geared to covering inefficiency and ineptness, to preserving old skills rather than developing better ones, to protecting practitioners from lay criticism or economic penalties for unsuccessful endeavors, to upgrading economic return by creating unnecessary scarcity in manpower, to demanding special privileges and exemptions from social controls which other professions might equally deserve.

[3] Greenwood, *op cit.*, 49–51.

While such possible abuses must be kept in mind in planning well-rounded education, and the new practitioner forewarned about them, such precautions should not overshadow the basic positive function of this part of the curriculum, to make the student aware that his profession serves a social purpose, that it is directed toward desirable ends, that its internal self-disciplinary measures have been formalized in order to insure the continued development of the profession. In short, one of the best protections against narrow professional interest will be a sense of the social usefulness and possibilities for service inherent in the chosen profession.

An ideal and recommended personal behavior, a commonly held goal, and agreed upon ways of achieving it, are seen by many scholars to be the very heart of the idea, "profession." For example, Ralph W. Tyler says:

> There is the existence of a recognized code of ethics . . . [which] commits the members of the profession to certain social values above the selfish ones of income, power and prestige . . . It expects the individual member seriously to dedicate himself to these higher values . . . A profession establishes some form of group discipline in support of these values.[4]

The professional ideal is used as a measure of the efficacy of all that a profession does; it attracts new entrants to whom the idea of its kind of service has special appeal; it gives the general public some sense of assurance that reliance on members of the profession is not misplaced. Most of all it is the chief bond which unites all members of the profession in common as well as individual activities. In contemplating becoming a member, in fulfilling society's expectations as he practices, in furthering its contribution by new discoveries, each member is motivated by the ideal of his profession. His obligations and special privileges are derived from it. Without it, he would be operating an individual technical enterprise; his commitment to it marks him as participating in a collective endeavor.

4 Ralph E. Tyler, "Educational Problems in Other Professions," in *Education for Librarianship* ed. by Bernard Berelson (Chicago: American Library Association, 1949), 22–23.

SOCIAL WORK ADAPTATION OF
THE SERVICE IDEAL

Social work has aspired to be a profession since the eighties and in an increasing crescendo has declared that it *is*. It has been no exception among professions in affirming that it stands *for* something, but has been atypical in that its ideal has been variously expressed and seldom pinpointed in one single encompassing goal. Yet author after author identifies one of social work's outstanding characteristics as its goal-centeredness, and sees the commitment to common values as a distinguishing trait and common bond.[5]

Despite difficulties with precise definitions there seems to be little doubt in the minds of practitioners representing all the professional specialities that social workers together are working toward some commonly held notions of how they would like to see society organized and social living conducted. This is a perceptible characteristic to people outside the profession who know social work intimately. For example, Charlotte Babcock observed that social workers had an ideal of their role as that of creating optimum conditions for full ego development, "to integrate the psychological needs of individuals with their societal needs." [6]

At least since 1920 [7] social workers singly and in specialized

[5] Examples of such statements are: Werner W. Boehm, "The Role of Values in Social Work," *The Jewish Social Service Quarterly*, XXVI, 4 (June, 1950), 429–438; Gordon Hamilton, "Helping People—The Growth of a Profession," in *Social Work as Human Relations* (New York: Columbia University Press, 1949), 3–18; Gordon Hamilton, *Theory and Practice of Social Casework*, 2nd ed. rev. (New York: Columbia University Press, 1951), 3, 6, 11, 38–43; Swithun Bowers, O.M.I., "Social Work and Human Problems," *Social Casework*, XXXV, 5 (May, 1954), 191; Mary Antoinette Cannon, "Guiding Motives in Social Work," in *New Directions in Social Work* ed. by Cora Kasius (New York: Harper & Bros., 1954), 13–30; Grace L. Coyle, *Group Experience and Democratic Values* (New York: Woman's Press, 1947); Kenneth L. M. Pray, "Social Work and Social Action," in *Proceedings of the National Conference of Social Work, 1945* (New York: National Conference of Social Work by Columbia University Press, 1945), 350–359; Gertrude Wilson and Gladys Ryland, *Social Group Work Practice* (Boston: Houghton, Mifflin Co., 1949), 16–22; Murray G. Ross, *Community Organization* (New York: Harper & Bros., 1955), 76–78.

[6] Charlotte Babcock, "The Social Worker in a World of Stress," *Social Service Review*, XXV, 1 (March, 1951), 1–13.

[7] "Experimental Draft of a Code of Ethics for Social Case Workers," [Authorship attributed to Mary E. Richmond. Printed but not published, ca. 1924.] (New York: Charity Organization Department, Russell Sage Foundation, now in Charity Organization Department Files, Archives, Library of the New York School of Social Work, Columbia University.)

groups have also been making attempts to describe ideal social work behavior in specific professional ethical principles and directives. Some of the most recent attempts are *Standards for the Professional Practice of Social Work* in 1951, "Group Workers and Professional Ethics," in 1953, and the Canadian "Code of Ethics." [8]

Analysts of the professional concept observe that in the process of inducting new members, the professional ideal and the approved and expected behavior patterns are an inescapable core which must be deliberately learned or subconsciously acquired through imitation and personal ego strivings to meet professional expectations. Every professional person must sense what his profession is trying to do, and, within tacitly understood or prescribed limits of variation, act as other members of the profession and the general public anticipate that he will act.[9]

It seems axiomatic that if social work is a heavily value-laden profession, its values also must be communicated to new recruits, and understood and accepted by them in their efforts to develop into *bona fide* professional representatives. If there are typical or required ways of behaving, a new social worker must be familiar with them, and exemplify them. Social work educators have followed general professional precedent in declaring this to be one of the desired results of professional education.

It is the opinion of the author that in social work, perhaps even more than in other professions, it is particularly essential that the idealistic underpinning as well as the scientific base in knowledge and acquired skills be communicated in the educational process. Because social work touches so many individual and social facets of human life, it is easy for a worker to lose his feeling of the ultimate purpose of his work. Specialization in areas of work associated

[8] American Association of Social Workers, *Standards for the Professional Practice of Social Work*, Supplement to July, 1952, *Social Work Journal*, Part II (New York: AASW, 1952); L. K. Hall, "Group Workers and Professional Ethics," *The Group*, XV, 1 (October, 1952), 3–8; Agnes Roy, "Code of Ethics," *The Social Worker*, XXIII, 1 (October, 1954), 4–7. The newly organized National Association of Social Workers is at present working on an enlarged ethical statement, National Association of Social Workers, Delegate Assembly *Workbook I*, Delegate Assembly *Workbook II* (New York: NASW, 1958).

[9] Towle, *op. cit.*, 10–17, 46–49; Arlien Johnson, "Educating Professional Social Workers for Ethical Practice," *Social Service Review*, XXIX, 2 (June, 1955), 125–126; Council on Social Work Education, *Manual of Accrediting Standards for Graduate Schools of Social Work* (New York: CSWE, revised as of May 1, 1957), section 352.

with each of its facets of interest has characterized the development of the social work profession as a whole. There is, thus, danger in tangential preoccupation with professional specialties to the exclusion of broad professional concerns, in failing to enhance one's own profession by greater identification with allied professions, and in becoming so enamored of the satisfactions of skilled performance that the long-range goals of the performance are lost sight of during its execution. Any professional person, if he is to have a balanced sense of what he is about, must perceive himself as one representative in a large vital endeavor, and relate his own behavior to what society and his fellow practitioners have so far defined as his essential contribution.

While we are teaching specific technical knowledge and inculcating a questioning and critical attitude toward past limitations and present imperfections in the helping process, it seems essential also to acquaint the future practitioner with the positive broader view, what the profession would like to do, has done and is doing. As social work is still in the process of refining the definitions of its essential purpose and of formulating behavior norms, educators have an opportunity to so adjust learning experiences that the dangers in too narrow self-preservative impulses are minimized while positive professional pride is developed.

ISSUES AND UNCERTAINTIES

Since value-laden goals and ethical behavior norms are accepted by most professions as prominent distinguishing features which must be transmitted to inductees, since social work seems to have followed this general professional pattern, and since social work educators are agreed this area of content is an educational responsibility, why has this aspect of professional preparation frequently been omitted from specific compilations of essential learning components?

Some of the reasons for this may be found in the following listing of a number of opinions expressed by faculty members in the course of this study. These questions or opinions were contributed in discussions, questionnaires and correspondence and were noted and analyzed by the project director as described in the chapter on method. They have been grouped into the following statements, each representing an issue which must be dealt with by any faculty planning its total curriculum and evaluated for its merits and questionable aspects. A brief critical evaluation based on other study materials accompanies each "point of view" as it is listed below.

1. *"There is no clearly defined, explicit demand for this material* from agencies absorbing the product of our schools. We do not yet know what values and ethical norms are of practical use."

Educational content must follow practice, so this group maintains, and social work has not identified its professional ideal with sufficient clarity to make a planned educational program feasible. There is much to back this opinion. Job descriptions, civil service examinations, specifications in requests for workers, seldom list philosophical and ethical equipment *as such*. A notable exception is the Family Service Association of America, which lists among desired abilities "to assume all the basic responsibilities inherent in professional practice as outlined in the Code of Ethics." [10]

Just why agencies have so far largely ignored this aspect of professional competence for job performance can only be speculated upon. Job specification statements seem to lean on formal definitions in terms of years of experience, progress of clientele during practice, estimates of superiors, and so on. Competence in the area of ethical perceptions is hard to define and measure. With the emphasis on needed self-knowledge and emotional development during the past twenty years, there may also have been a tendency to regard value formation as an inseparable aspect of a worker's internal personality, overlooking cultural and group origins and elements of professional identification. Since the *Manual of Accrediting Standards* and other educational norm descriptions *do* list familiarity with professional values and ethics, possibly, requirement of graduation from an approved school may often be assumed to cover this aspect of professional mastery. For instance, the recom-

[10] Family Service Association of America, *A Guide to Classification of Professional Positions and Evaluation Outlines in a Family Service Agency* (New York: FSAA, 1957), 11.

mendation of the Southern Regional Education Board of "at least one full year of graduate social work education . . . and full professional education . . . for certain positions" was expanded to say that this would assure recognition by staff that "people have potentialities which may be realized if given appropriate opportunities," one of social work's most frequently verbalized values.[11]

A detailed study of practice, including an examination of the values, underlying assumptions and goals, and ethical principles operating in professional judgment, is highly essential to an economical (in time and student effort) educational program. Lacking such a formulation, the author drew from all the data of the study and listed separately each description of or reference to a situation in practice in which orientation to value and ethical concepts seemed to have been an important aspect of effective professional performance.[12] Sources of such data included cases used in teaching, treatises on social work methodology and philosophy, statements made in class audits describing good practice, descriptions of good and poor field performance in student evaluations (the most fruitful source). All the situations showed that social work practice involves continuous consideration of competing or conflicting value positions.

All social work behavior is a process of making choices; some become self-evident and semi-automatic to the experienced professional worker, but represent a long development of value selection on the part of many practitioners, with which each new entrant must experiment and whose validity he must discover for himself. Study of these behavior situations indicated that there are typical choices a professional worker repeatedly makes, some behaviors he approves, some he disapproves. Many situations, much more difficult, indicate that crucial social work decisions often hinge on choice between several theoretically desirable or approved courses of action.

From a grouping and rough classification of these materials,

11 Ellen Winston, "Sounder Public Welfare Programs Through Adequate Staffing," *Public Welfare News*, XX, 1 (North Carolina State Department of Public Welfare, March, 1957), 1.
12 See Chapter II for descriptions of this methodology. Out of these situation descriptions grew the objectives, Chapter V.

collected from such diverse sources, the ten major educational objectives were derived, a list of desirable professional ways of behaving requiring familiarity with professional positions as to values and ethics. The list was reviewed by the Panel on Values and Ethics, whose members agreed that these behaviors are an essential part of professional performance and it was felt that even without confirmation from a systematic study of practice, the usefulness of such knowledge could be assumed, and definite plans should be made for developing such behavior in students.

2. *"Social work values are not in any way distinctive* from those any good person in our North American culture would hold. While social agencies want their staff members to be value conscious and ethical on their jobs, this is largely provided for by the process of growing up in a democratic society such as that to which professional entrants have long been exposed."

It appears to be true that many of the values which social work affirms had their origins in Judaeo-Christian religious beliefs and Anglo-American political and legal philosophies. However, these permeating value traditions take on a variety of forms, and each member of society makes his particular interpretation of them, and ranks them in importance out of his own experiences. The occupational and national backgrounds of his parents, the sectional culture patterns of the community in which he grew up, the income and educational status of his family, all modify these germinal sources of ideas. One student said in an interview, "Sure I always believed in the Bible. I did a lot of church welfare work and I always voted, but here I saw the same good old ideas the way they could work out with all kinds of people. They aren't just the same when a social worker starts applying them. They are *real;* you have to work at them; you can't lazily take them for granted as you always had."

One of the current lay critics of the profession has commented that "the most endearing trait of social workers is the fact that they really mean what they say about the importance of the individual." And, "the explicitness with which social workers practice what they preach tends to jolt those accustomed only to the more abstract manifestations of democracy." [13] The student social worker must learn *how* social workers "mean it," the social work interpretation and application of value principles to specific human situations. In the opinion of the author the student records examined indicate that general acculturation is a foundation on which the specifics of social work may be developed, but cannot be trusted to provide an ever present working philosophic approach. To use one example, "democracy" may mean enforced rule of the majority to some people in our culture, while to the social worker it may mean recognition of minority aspirations and places for minority participation. Similarly "justice" may mean social vindication through punishment to some members of our culture or a second chance by re-educational methods to others.

3. *"Value orientation is largely a matter of student selection.* Values and a 'sense of the ethical' are learned early in life as part of the interactive process in socialization. The broad culture, as such, cannot be trusted because of the variations in exposure and interpretation, but social work schools can seek specific cultural exposures among applicants to meet professional needs."

In the Curriculum Study we have assumed that schools will always make careful selection of students, which involves attention to attitude formation as part of their personal equipment. Studies of prediction of success in the learning experience confirm that this is probably possible of execution. However, as with the general culture, study of student progress in records read makes one question whether selection can be relied upon to insure that all needed or desirable positions with respect to values are evenly developed, or that they are grasped in such form as to be readily used in performance. A student whose first year record was uniformly superior commented, "I was brainwashed and I am grateful, though I would have said I agreed with every bit when I came." Questions of level of understanding and the breadth of possibilities for applying philosophic assumptions have to be dealt with in the kinds of decision-making episodes of which the every day social work situa-

[13] Marion K. Sanders, "Social Work: A Profession Chasing Its Tail," *Harper's Magazine,* CCXIV (March, 1957), 59.

tion consists. Previous commitments to compatible values may make their specific application easier, but cannot replace the wrestling with such problems in a social work context.

4. *"Values and ethical norms will be learned regardless of any specific planning* because they are an integral, inseparable part of social work. They cannot be distilled out as an entity; any attempt at exact definition defeats its purpose. A value is lost whenever an attempt is made to examine it. Values and ethics belong to that part of human experience which is a by-product of living. Satisfactory professional value orientation and knowledge of professionally approved and disapproved behavior are a certain by-product of exposure to social work activity and theoretical formulation."

Voluminous materials available to this project indicated that the whole educational process is pervaded with content involving value judgments and ethical considerations. No class which was audited lacked reference to some value position. Every piece of student material, examinations, papers, and theses, included value assumptions or listings of values. Every supervisory and faculty evaluative statement illustrated use of values and ethics in field teaching. Questionnaires indicated that the entire range of courses was planned to help create awareness of the importance of values.

Where there was, however, no specific effort on the part of faculty to insure systematic introduction and inclusion of such material, it appeared that some useful and much needed content might be omitted with respect to any single student. Depending on the particular faculty members to whom he was exposed, the field material he personally confronted in practice, the priority value judgments and interests of his field teachers, and his own inclinations in suggested or optional assignments, an individual student might nearly or wholly escape personal exposure to certain classic social work decisions and points of view. For example, a student whose experience was entirely with intensive one-to-one relationships focused on single clients was highly disturbed by an implication coming late in his fourth semester that his professional obligations extended to evaluating the effect of treatment on a client's family and surrounding community.

Another, three weeks before graduation, had never heard of the pamphlet, *Standards for the Professional Practice of Social Work.* In that particular school, a number of teachers in different courses referred to it, but check confirmed that probably none of his particular teachers had customarily used it. Chief reliance for knowledge of the activity of the National Association of Social Workers rested on student membership (completely optional with no pressure or consistent recruitment). Membership had been adjudged too expensive by this student.

Judging from student statements and faculty evaluations of student performance in class and field, the single most effective learning experience for value formation and use appeared to be "exposure to the social work atmosphere," but less painful and more certain learning appeared to take place when elements in the atmosphere were periodically checked and evaluated by faculty, with some aspects deliberately planned. Some overall, definitely understood plan for introduction of a major framework of value ideas insured that a minimum of by-product learning would occur, even though under lack of any plan most students could be expected to learn much successfully.

Trusting to "exposure" involved danger of fragmentation. One value would be stressed, while its corollary or related concepts were only lightly touched on, if at all. There seemed to be much more stress on individual "right" than social responsibility and interdependence. "Acceptance" might be taught without reference to "limits." A balanced overall conception of values to be taken into consideration in decision-making seemed to require concerted, focused attention to both formal and informal learning.

5. *"Values and ethical decisions are wholly a matter of individual choice* on the part of each social worker and each social agency. Each cultural sub-group within our larger American culture, and throughout the world, has its own value orientation. Each social worker must select from a myriad of value systems that which is congenial and meaningful for him; schools have an obligation *not* to teach in such a highly personal area. Each consuming agency will ultimately judge whether each social worker's approach meets the ethical norms of that particular agency."

This point of view might be regarded as a *laissez-faire* handling of the philosophic components in social work. "Indocrination," "inculcation," "manipulation" were words invested by faculty members with a negative feeling to express deep concerns about the ethical right of a school of social work to make any organized attempt to teach values and ethics.

On the other hand, use as negative criticism of the phrase "persistent lay attitudes" in evaluation of students having more than usual difficulty and in faculty conferences would lead to the inference that by the end of the fourth semester educators do, in fact, expect a student to have acquired some specific points of view that can be regarded as suitably "professional." The term was usually undefined, either in examples or explanation, implying unquestioned assumptions of what ought to exist attitudinally. The positive presence of acceptable attitudes in "good" students was less frequently noted except in phrases such as "excellent identification with the goals and ethics of the profession."

If we actually have such negative and positive behavior expectations for the beginning practitioner on an operational level, must educators not take responsibility for exposing him to "desirable" ways of thinking or commending attitudes which conform to social work demands? If we genuinely believed that every worker must select value positions on his own, would we not be under obligation to accept whatever he discovered to be compatible with his conception of social work? These evaluations indicated that in all eight schools studied, there was a quite settled notion, both negatively and positively, of disvalues and a fairly definite formulation of essential values which are regarded as indispensable. Schools showed a great similarity in the values stressed most often. While, ultimately, it would be anticipated that each worker would annex these values as part of the experience of having a professional self, and make them completely his own, it appeared that all schools actually teach values, and that the learning of them is facilitated by forthright acknowledgment that they are being taught.

Each of these issues must be re-examined continuously and some kind of decision made regarding it before learning experiences can be devised. Curriculum planners must ask:

Do we have a clear idea of what to teach without the much needed analysis of practice?

Can we trust general cultural exposure?

Can we provide required value orientation through student selection process alone?

Will value learning be an inevitable by-product of our other activities without specific provisions for it?

Are value commitments wholly a matter for student decision unaided by faculty influence?

It is the belief of this author that the evidence produced by schools all over the country suggests that social work has reached tentative formulations of its values sufficient to make introduction of formal learning in this area feasible and productive. Early experiences and exposure to the "social work culture" predispose to satisfactory learning, but cannot be regarded as sufficient and certain to meet the demands of effective social work performance.

CHAPTER II

Methodology and Nature of Data

In common with the methods of all the projects and the central design of the Curriculum Study, the design of this project placed primary emphasis on content analysis of a wide range of materials and on review and consultation by panels.

Having decided that because of limitations in time and lack of previously assembled materials the project would have to be conducted on an extensive, exploratory rather than a highly detailed level, the following preliminary definition of scope was developed with the help of the staff and the *Ad Hoc* Panel on Definitions.

SCOPE OF PROJECT

This study is to be concerned with the educational arrangements by which a member of the social work profession can be equipped to approach practice situations in which he will confront choices among values to all of which the profession generally would subscribe. These choices involve an understanding of the process by which values are formulated, knowledge of formal and informal prescriptions, the recognition of situations in which there are alternatives, and final decision making and implementation.

Since we are a practicing profession, the ultimate concern of social work educators is not with the intellectual ability to define value and ethical principles, nor with the student's willingness to affirm them verbally, but with the student's capacity to recognize when the application of an ethical norm would be indicated, how principles can be made clear to others on an action level, and how a value may be applied in the ethical handling of himself.[1]

1 This statement is a modification of one appearing in the original research design for this project through suggestions made by the *Ad Hoc* Panel and by the staff.

WORKING DEFINITIONS[2]

Terms used to express value and ethical ideas are varied and no two experts agree on them. In order to have a systematic manner of handling assembled data, tentative descriptive formulations were made, and reviewed by the *Ad Hoc* Panel of professional philosophers, representing many points of view. While individually each member might have added qualifying or expansive phrases, there was consensus that the following statements should enable the project director to determine when value or ethical content was being confronted.

VALUES

Values are formulations of preferred behavior held by individuals or social groups. They imply a usual preference for certain means, ends, and conditions of life, often being accompanied by strong feeling. While behavior may not always be consistent with values held, possession of values results in strain toward consistent choice of certain types of behavior whenever alternatives are offered. The meaning attached to values is of such impelling emotional quality that individuals who hold them often make personal sacrifices and work hard to maintain them, while groups will mobilize around the values they hold to exert approval and disapproval in the form of rewards and penalties (sanctions). Long repeated preferences often result in the feeling that what is preferred is intrinsically and indubitably "preferable." Values may be expressed in the negative as "disvalues" or prohibitions, formulations of behaviors to be avoided.

Although values may be expressed in abstract generalizations such as "democracy" or "personal independence," they are directly applicable to specific overt human behavior. The abstract expression of a value is oftentimes confused with the desired behavior pattern *per se,* as for instance, "democracy" in a small group with the agreed upon custom for group members to vote on a choice of

2 Definitions first formulated for the research design were reviewed by an *Ad Hoc* Panel on Definitions, modifications being in line with staff and panel suggestions.

program. In this study, great care must be taken to distinguish between the abstract value and the minute institutional forms in which it finds expression. There could well be agreement on an underlying "value" and disagreement as to which institution is best suited to achieve it and as to whether or not certain types of individual behavior exemplify it. Philosophically these distinctions are termed "ultimate" or "consummate" and "instrumental" or "proximate" values.

At least two types of values are frequently referred to in social work literature, "social values" and "spiritual values" (of which "religious values" are a sub-type). "Social values" refer to prescriptions of ideal behavior between individuals or groupings of individuals. "Spiritual values" prescribe behavior related to things which cannot be objectively verified by the senses, such as explanation of the mysteries of the universe, development of theistic ideas or rejections of such ideas, relationship between individuals and the universe as a whole, ideas concerning the origin and purpose of life, the meaning of beauty, compassion, etc.

ETHICS

The word "ethics" is used in two somewhat different senses, but the two are so interrelated that the distinction is rarely made.

1. The field or discipline of ethics concerns itself with the fulfillment of the human personality and ideal ends of human action, expressed in terms such as "good" and "bad," "right" and "wrong," "better" and "worse." It seeks to determine criteria by which to formulate ultimate social goals, to choose between conflicting or competing values, and to determine which should have priority.

2. The results of such considerations are sometimes gathered together as a body of principles referred to as "the ethics" or "ethic" (of a group, nation, profession, etc.). Even more specifically they may be reduced to detailed prescriptions, such as "codes."

"Ethical" behavior is behavior selected according to some common understanding as to what has been formally or informally adjudged "ideal" or "good," following approved principles or priorities by which selection among different "good" behaviors is made. "Ethics" thus refers both to the process by which ideals are established and to the product of the process. In using the term, care should be taken to indicate which sense it is to express in each context.

In addition to these two basic definitions, the project director collected a list of words [3] used in social work technical treatises offered as assignments, words used by teachers and students in classes audited, and words in project questionnaires and correspondence which seemed to express values or ethical prescriptions as defined above. From the context of the words on this list, assumed or implied meanings were noted. This list served as a social work vocabulary in the value-ethical field. Whenever these words were employed, the project director was alerted that value material might be involved. It became apparent that some of these words are used in somewhat differing ways, and yet there was surprising consistency in the general notions teachers and students were trying to convey. This part of the study was the basis for the formulations regarding semantic problems in Chapter III.

Throughout the gathering of data and analysis of findings, an attempt was made not to sway or alter current semantic usage but to find common ways in which a minimum number of social work commitments could be expressed. Every effort was made to distinguish between consistent application of the working definitions to detect values latent in curriculum materials and the discovery of understandings and habitual usage in professional communication, educational, and practice situations. This report itself has had to be expressed in what seem to the author the most frequent and meaningful terms current in the literature. The *Ad Hoc* Panel advised that exact definition of every term in words acceptable to every social worker was virtually impossible, for value and ethical ideas can be expressed only in other words of equally vague and shifting meaning. Very early in the study it became apparent that the materials dealt with in this project could not be handled with the same degree of objectivity and consistency that can be achieved with legal, medical, and historical information and hypotheses. This is an area where personal emotional impressions, speculation, and human sensitivity necessarily influence practice performance,

3 See Appendix D, "List of Words Encountered."

but are so individual that insistence on absolutely uniform approaches would have no validity. To have any meaning for the planning of social work education the speculative and esoteric nature of the materials used has to be accepted as a realistic, if difficult, governing factor. To compress content too rigidly seemed to defeat the very purpose of the exploration. Philosophic, anthropological and sociological literature at present contains many discussions as to whether values are so elusive as to be subjects not suited to standard research procedures. At the beginning of this study, the author made the assumption that possibly something could be learned about the values of social work, but that any discoveries probably would not have the explicit quality desirable in other areas of content.

SOURCES OF DATA

Every piece of data was looked at with respect to what it had to offer in the way of answering three types of questions. Almost every source yielded information on each, but in varying degree.

1. What are the characteristics of the social work value system and ethical approaches to practice? What formulations are fairly consistently accepted as typical of social work goals and working assumptions? How are they applied?

2. What are the learning problems peculiar to value and ethics, in general and in social work?

3. What can experiences in graduate schools of social work suggest as to desirable learning consistent with educational difficulties and professional needs? Where and how in the curriculum have values heretofore been learned?

Items related to these three major considerations, plus all words used in describing or explaining them, were tabulated on separate slips and later hand grouped in general types of problems, out of which the objectives were eventually formulated. Classifications grew out of the material and were not anticipated in any proposed or hypothetical groupings.

Because it was anticipated that the entire learning experience should be examined, eight schools were selected for observation of the total experience to which students were exposed.[4] Special attention was paid to the relatedness with which value material occurred in different courses, and to "atmospheric" learning. The eight schools were selected because of their accessibility to New York, but included public and private, non-sectarian and sectarian [5] sponsorship; variations in size and age of school; and variations in type of community. No attempt was made to construct a scientific sample of all schools. Material secured, therefore, is in no sense a sampling of all education now being carried on and was regarded only as suggestive and illustrative.

On visits to the assisting schools, faculty members were interviewed singly and in groups, curriculum materials examined, classes audited, selected student evaluations read, and students interviewed. (The subsequent descriptions of types of material collected give some idea of the general approach.)

In order to amplify this rather narrow source of data, and to provide opportunity for extensive as well as intensive analysis, a questionnaire was devised and sent to all accredited graduate schools of social work.

To make sure that current social work opinion was represented, four standard works assigned frequently for student reading were analyzed in sentence by sentence manner, four entire copies of social work periodicals for one month were examined similarly, and twelve other works frequently assigned were less intensively perused through such techniques as examination of index.

Educational materials such as workshop and committee reports, catalogues, course descriptions, and discussions of curriculum committees were used for further exploration of thinking.

---

4 List of Schools:
  Adelphi College, School of Social Work
  Catholic University of America, National Catholic School of Social Service
  Fordham University, School of Social Service
  Howard University, Graduate School of Social Work
  New York School of Social Work of Columbia University
  New York University, Graduate School of Public Administration and Social Service
  University of Connecticut, School of Social Work
  University of Pennsylvania, School of Social Work
5 The only sectarian schools used here were Catholic schools, but conceivably there might be others in the future to which similar principles would apply.

CLASS AUDIT

A total of 31 classes were audited, as follows:

Philosophy, Ethics, "The Profession," "Basic Concepts"	9
Casework Method (I, II, IV)	5
Group Work Method (I, II, Advanced)	5
Community Organization Method	2
Social Services	5
Human Growth and Behavior	5

These classes were selected in consultation with the deans of the assisting schools. An effort was made to audit at least one class in each school in which the curriculum plan of the school anticipated that values and ethics would be introduced explicitly, such as "Ethics," "History and Philosophy," "The Profession," "Cultural Influences," "Issues in Social Work." Other courses were selected according to what was being given at the time of the visit and subjective impressions that certain teachers either stressed philosophic teaching, had been particularly successful with it, or had done provocative experimentation in method or content. The remainder were added in order to include as many methods and specializations as possible. There is no way of determining how typical or representative of the schools, or of social work teaching as a whole these particular sessions may have been. They produced suggestive material concerning included content, level of abstraction in presentation, problems in student reaction and understanding, and professional expectations of the behavior of the "good" social worker.

These audits confirmed the hypothesis that value material is contained in all courses. They revealed the importance of teacher attitude and of the manner in which material is presented. In some sessions there was frequent reference to the fact that what was being presented was similar to content students had met or would encounter in other courses. In other sessions there seemed to be a tendency to present a principle commonly considered to be applicable throughout the profession as something dealing only with the specific situation or method under discusson. Audits underscored the need for faculty agreement on responsibility for integration in the curriculum.

An unexpected result of class audits was discovery of the need students felt to find a middle range of abstraction.[6] They seemed to be satisfied neither with high level abstractions such as "democracy," "acceptance," and so on, nor with discussing material exclusively from the situational point of view. This led to further examination of terms customarily used and to the conclusion that this range of terminology should be the subject of experimentation and more detailed research.

As a whole, the audits furnished a cumulative impression of many of the issues, and the general nature of social work approaches to ethical and value implications in practice. Descriptive material concerning present handling was largely drawn from audits, supplemented by teacher accounts of classroom episodes in the questionnaire and written descriptions by one of the assisting schools. An attempt at a schedule of items to be considered in listening was given up after experimentation because much significant material was difficult to foresee and was being lost. As complete a chronological note-taking as possible was substituted, classification of items following. It was found that many unanticipated suggestive materials emerged in this unstructured approach. If a definitive study of teaching practices and class content in this area were to be made, a pilot study of forty to sixty audits probably would be necessary before any systematic system of notation could be devised.

Audits illustrated that many of the values of social work are communicated by interaction between teacher and pupil and between pupil and pupil. They made clear the difficulty of separating method and content in this type of material.

If time during school visits had permitted, audits would have been a fruitful resource which might have been used to a larger extent. There should have been audits during both semesters in each school to give a full picture of curriculum integration.

STUDENT MATERIAL

Papers were read from history, philosophy, ethics, social work seminar, casework, group work, basic concepts and methods, administration, and research courses. One student analysis of the

6 See Chapter III for details of findings.

values derived from field work was included. These were suggested by teachers, usually in interviews. Minutes of three social work seminars were read. Five student theses were read in entirety.

All these sources indicated the terminology in which students were learning to express values, the values most often stressed, areas of student confusion, reluctance to accept, or conflict of values. The problem brought up most often was the sectarian agency, which seemed in conflict with the principle of acceptance of all people. Limitation of clientele, not auspices, was the chief concern. The application of a non-judgmental attitude when the social worker had definite standards of behavior in mind was next often mentioned. Other problems of ethical nature were: how to integrate outer and inner needs of one person; how to balance responsibilities to the individual and to associated others (group members, family, neighborhood); the social worker's responsibility to initiate social action or accept the community where it is; acceptance of agency policy which was in conflict with principles of minimum adequate meeting of survival needs; the social worker's responsibility in a setting practicing a punitive or authoritarian approach; in such settings, how far a social worker can accept the authority of other disciplines.

These papers stimulated consideration of whether we often teach abstract values outside the context where they are applied, or without mentioning other values of opposite import which also are accepted by social work.

STUDENT INTERVIEWS

The research design did not provide for direct interviewing of students. Unexpectedly, it was found that in every school visit, students sought out the project director after the purpose of the visit was announced in class. These interviews (34) were completely informal. It was not always possible to ascertain names or check with faculty as to whether these particular students were having normal or unusual difficulty. On those that could be checked, all but one were described as superior students. These unsought comments without exception indicated enthusiasm for explicit teaching of values and ethics and a desire for more. They also indicated a pervasive student impression that verbalization and practice are not integrated, that values are considered singly without relation to others, and especially that field situations and class material are not sufficiently related. Student interviews underscored the importance of "atmosphere" and observational impressions.

For a definitive study, a more systematic interviewing of students should be provided for in the design. The kind of material produced spontaneously would indicate doubt that an instrument, such as a questionnaire or attitude measurement test would reveal as much as unstructured interviews, but pilot studies along these lines ought to be attempted.

While material from student contacts is highly charged emotionally, fragmentary, and in no sense selected on a representative basis, it appeared to be so thought-provoking that it was included as descriptive and suggestive for further analysis. For example, the most consistent student complaint about class teaching was that they felt faculty members did not accept students' questions in a value area as being philosophic and speculative, but usually interpreted them narrowly as manifestations of personal conflict. Students called attention to two sources of confusion: the difference between culture, generally referred to, and values; and the failure, in value expectations of students, to distinguish between internalized personality organization and external adaptations to cultural variations.

FACULTY INTERVIEWS, CONFERENCES, AND
WRITTEN MATERIAL FROM SCHOOLS

In the beginning after an informal request for personal opinion about effective teaching in this area, an attempt was made to interview faculty members according to a schedule which included items mentioned in the research design. It was found that many members had difficulty in focusing on value and ethical material specifically. Therefore, interviews (50) were directed to discussing content in course outlines and audits, and faculty members were encouraged to think of recent examples in class and field instruction where values and ethics had entered into the teaching process, and to tell about bits of effective learning they had witnessed or heard about.

The most helpful sources of suggestions as to objectives and content came from the nine group discussions. One member of a faculty would stimulate another to think of illustrations and material that should be included. Discussion of student evaluations that were being read led to attempts to verbalize expectations for students, and elicited examples of student learning difficulties.

Accounts of experiments in the teaching of values at the different schools such as observational trips, mixing of student specialties in class formation, structured and unstructured seminars, promotion of various student activities, helped the director consider what content was essential, and again made clear the difficulty of distinguishing between content and method in an area where effective learning often takes place in unplanned and unverbalized communication. Due to lack of time on visits, field teachers were not seen as much as would have been desirable.

As a whole, faculty members were much more prepared to discuss the teaching of abstract value formulations than to hazard opinion about teaching ethics. This seemed to be a reflection of the primitive and generalized state of professional ethical formulations. The lack of teaching materials was mentioned frequently. In schools where it was possible to revisit, the project director found many faculty members had saved up pertinent episodes to relate. A number of written accounts were also collected.

In addition to the eight assisting schools, course materials sent to the Study on the total curriculum of ten schools were examined. Any mention of value or ethical material and objectives was noted, and each one contributed to the final formulation of desirable objectives.

All catalogues were scanned for generalized value statements (goals, objectives, etc.) and descriptions of courses which indicated *specific* teaching of values were noted (ethics, philosophy, "the profession," "the agency," etc.). All courses mentioned in questionnaires as attempting to teach values *as such* were scanned similarly.

QUESTIONNAIRES

Thirty-four schools responded to a questionnaire sent to all accredited graduate schools.[7] Of these, one had twenty faculty members respond individually, representing all parts of the curriculum, and these responses were incorporated with those of the assisting schools. The questionnaire was designed to elicit faculty opinion concerning what are major professional values and descriptions of current teaching practice. One of its major objectives was to determine how the profession at present uses the terms "values" and "ethics." Another objective was to test whether there is, as yet, any uniform or typical conception of what behavior is ethical or non-ethical, whether we are moving toward "principles," and any consistent opinion as to where professional people would place priorities if two approved values conflicted.

Since sociological, anthropological and professional philosophical literature all indicated that verbalized goals, or what a group would like to accomplish, seem to be the best single indication of the values they hold, schools were asked to list goals. Answers were exceedingly suggestive for formulation of educational objectives, for study of semantic difficulties, and for formulation of professional value concepts. In spite of varying verbal usage, answers showed wide consensus on major conceptual positions, and particularly brought out that any teaching of values must come to grips with how to resolve simultaneous concern for the individual and for larger social groupings.

A part of the questionnaire was addressed to two major assumptions to be examined: (1) that primary focus should be placed on teaching how to apply values in an ethical manner in situations where choice between conflicting values is confronted, and (2) that such learning very likely takes place in all parts of the curriculum. Schools were asked in what ways their students might have learned how to handle themselves in twelve problems from practice, each corresponding superficially to one of the statements in the *Standards for the Professional Practice of Social Work*. These practice problems were formulated by the project director from occurrences in field work, descriptions in literature, and known episodes in practice.

Answers to these situations, as had been hoped, were highly individual in approach. They showed the difficulties in any attempts at generalization. They were the best source of information on our current semantic usage and on values which are operational

7 See Appendix B for copy of Questionnaire.

in nature,[8] and indicate that as yet the profession has not arrived at any compilation which can be considered uniformly applicable in specific confrontations of choice. (See Appendix C for a sample answer to one question.)

On the whole, replies to questionnaires indicated that the entire curriculum was permeated with value teaching and showed some of the special applications of value theory for which each part of the curriculum is best suited. They were the source of many suggestions on useful teaching materials.

STUDENT EVALUATIONS

Faculties in assisting schools were asked to suggest records of student progress for students considered superior in performance at time of graduation and also for students who were marginal or having unusual difficulty. Sixty-three records on graduates of June 1956 were used, thirty-five "good," twenty-eight "poor." Final evaluation statements in these records were read to determine what our expectations are at time of graduation insofar as they relate to values and ethics. Student progress from time of application was then followed, to locate any learning experiences which seemed to have contributed to these results. From one school to another records vary to such extent in form and in semantic usage that the best comparisons were those between the two groups of students in the same school. Expectations were very similar in all schools, and formed the most fruitful source for objectives. Every school mentioned characteristics (negatively or positively) that conform to each of these objectives. The most praised characteristic was "ability to understand and work with all kinds of people." The most frequent criticism was "still retains some lay attitudes." There was no discernible difference in expectations from students in different methods and specialties.

Much of the material about values to be learned in field practice came from reports of field teachers incorporated in student records.

PROCESS OF DATA ANALYSIS

For analysis, materials from all sources were combined into a single set of data for considering each of the major questions. Separate

8 See Chapter III.

analyses were made of expectations as shown in evaluations, of semantic usage, and of responses to social work situations that appeared to require orientation to values and ethics. These separate sub-studies confirmed the results of the undifferentiated analysis with respect to formation of objectives and added little illumination except for illustrative purposes.

In the preliminary analytic process, some sixty (depending on wording used) possible objectives were siphoned from all suggestions accumulated. These were grouped and regrouped until the present list (see page 5) was compiled. The objectives thus arranged were checked to see whether all social work situations listed had been provided for, whether all goals listed in questionnaires were included, whether the main expectations indicated in evaluations were covered, and whether they were compatible with the literature data analysis.

Objectives were then reviewed by the Study staff for suggestions on wording and clarification.

A panel of educators and practitioners spent two days reviewing and commenting on the objectives. Originally there had been subdivisions which the Panel suggested might be eliminated. The Panel also contributed social work material which could illustrate the implementation of objectives, and assisted in the consideration of course content which might help achieve them. Because the Panel was selected from a limited geographic area, a Panel of correspondents was asked to review the objectives and comment further.

Findings from all these analyses and reviews have been organized (as they appear now in the two following chapters) both from the standpoint of professional practice and from the standpoint of the learner. By simultaneous coordination of the values thus revealed as the profession's aim for its practitioners and the value structure and learning process typical of the student, the desirable educational objectives listed in Chapter V were formulated.

Devising learning experiences to attain these objectives is the primary responsibility of each school faculty. However, in the course of this study, some possible principles emerged for organizing and ordering this material in a curriculum, which are briefly discussed in Chapter VI as tentative suggestions brought out by the study process.

In dealing with such elusive, pervasive, difficult-to-define material, the researcher finds himself accumulating impressions, no one of which is decisively significant in and of itself, but which *in toto* seem to point to possibilities. Articles and books had to be read for their total contribution rather than by sections or separate ideas, and the danger was recognized of quotation out of context, or partial development of themes the authors intended to be complete. It is, therefore, hard always to assign the source of each idea herein contained, even though they grew out of the research process, and often differ from the author's original hunches and positions. Also, in securing data from the assisting schools, the promise was made that all interviews, evaluations, class episodes, and audits would be kept confidential and results would appear in pooled rather than specific form. Since the research process thus makes individual credit for germinal ideas impossible, the author hopes each contributing faculty member and student will be able to see where his own idea fitted into the whole. The give and take of faculty discussions and class sessions, comments in evaluations, and student comments have been used more often in formulating this summary of findings than has already written social work literature. Hence, credit for ideas can be ascribed only to the generosity of cooperating teachers and students, in many instances. The highly personal impressionistic nature of much of the material must be kept in mind in reading the report, for, undoubtedly, biases and preconceptions of the project director influenced selection and appraisal of what was recorded and used, in spite of constant conscious effort to record opinions as she understood contributors meant them to reach the professional stream of thought.

CHAPTER III

The Characteristics of Social Work Values and Ethics: How They Occur in the Learning Process

Before developing objectives it was necessary to consider the current state of value formation in social work. The educational process can sometimes anticipate trends in practice but cannot be far ahead of (or behind) the understanding of the body of current practitioners, if the student is to be enabled to work and communicate in the present structure.

SEMANTICS

One is immediately confronted with problems of communicating meaning, of definition, and of customary usage, both lay and professional. In teaching, these problems are not as simple as they can be made in research, where a meaning can be selected and used consistently.

Value words are employed constantly in everyday speech and assume subtle connotations for each individual, so that each person tends to read in his own habitual interpretations and to prefer his own usage, regardless of agreed-upon meaning. To "like" one thing better than another and to want it for himself or others is a common human experience expressed in an array of words indicating desired and undesired experiences and objects. To the person listening, words may have additional overtones of which the speaker may be unaware. Scholars who have studied the problem sometimes give up trying to form exact definitions, and all recognize the difficulty of making sure that the idea intended is actually communicated.[1] Any value usually can be defined only in other

[1] *E.g.*, Lee says, "I speak of value but I am not prepared to define it." Dorothy Lee, "Are Basic Needs Ultimate?" in *Personality in Nature, Society, and Culture* ed. by Clyde Kluckhohn and Henry A. Murray, 2nd ed. rev. (New York: Alfred A. Knopf, 1953), 335–341. Also see Charles Morris, *Varieties of Human Value* (Chicago: University of Chicago Press, 1956), 9–12.

value terms equally prone to varied meaning, carrying their own load of overtones and nuances.[2] Perhaps the simplest way of thinking is to think of what the individual or group would like to see happen; what their conception of an ideal world may be; what they would preserve from the present and what they would change if given the power to do so; what they take for granted as proper or to be expected; how they think society *should* be organized, what individuals *should* be like, what kinds of personality and conduct they wish could be developed in all people.[3] Given a conception of what should be, groups and individuals tend to choose means and modes of life which will help achieve the things they conceive as ideal and a system or constellation of preferences emerges.

Values are so often thought of as "the best"[4] that frequently they are implied or assumed without direct reference to them, when a course of action is being determined. As a practicing profession, whose members are constantly weighing "what to do," many of the social workers' values tend to go unspoken through assumed agreement as to the basis of a contemplated action. Students may make assumptions based on their habitual value orientation which do not coincide with a field or class teacher's intended implications. Two social workers in consultation may have slightly different conceptions of the same value to which both refer.[5]

In order not to sway customary social work usage by imposing the definitions essential for a research process, in the questionnaires faculties were asked to state what goals they most often stressed and to describe the values they found implicit in typical social work situations. Each member of the faculty of one of the larger assisting schools was also asked to describe current examples

2 See Classified Bibliography, Semantics and Communication Problems.
3 Two student attempts to define and study the nature of values are found in Hubert Eugene Jones, "An Exploratory Study of Social Work Values in Relation to Social Work Practice" (Unpublished Master's essay, School of Social Work, Boston University, 1957); Harriet R. Shur and Joyce Shutters, "A Study in Attitudes and Values of a Group of Second Year Students at the New York School of Social Work" (Unpublished Master's project, New York School of Social Work, Columbia University, 1956).
4 Clyde Kluckhohn and Henry A. Murray (eds.), *Personality in Nature, Society, and Culture* (2nd ed. rev. and enlarged; New York: Alfred A. Knopf, 1953), "Personality Formation: The Determinants," 59; Morris, *op. cit.*
5 Instances of such phenomena were described in supervisory accounts of field problems, in student evaluation records, and in student accounts in class sessions of their current practice problems.

of the teaching of values in his classes. From these statements it became clear that most teachers use value terms common in our democratic culture to describe social work's value implications and commitments.[6] These terms are the same ones encountered in preambles to legal documents, patriotic editorials, political speeches, and religious articles. Many attempted listings of social work values in professional literature confirm that this is true.[7] It poses an educational problem for social work—that of making glibly used idealistic words with loose meaning carry specialized and relatively consistent conceptual and operational connotations for guidance in developing a professional approach to the making of professional choices.

The terms "ethics" and "ethical" may have more definite connotation than "value," "democracy," "self-maximation," and so on, but they also are hard to define and elastic in application to specific situations. Social work literature and general usage indicate that "ethics" may be thought of both as a discipline and a code, and this causes problems in working out the interrelation of professional "values" and "ethics." Although there are many philosophic positions on this distinction, the advisory panel agreed that there are interacting influences between values and ethics, especially in the ethics and values of a small, relatively cohesive group like a profession. Ethics thought of as a philosophic discipline which determines what is "right" and "wrong" helps develop principles by which values, "what is preferred or best," are selected. These accepted values, in turn, influence what a group may codify as indisputably its ethical norms for right and wrong conduct. According to the ethics developed by the discipline, the values of some groups may be "unethical." According to cherished values held by some groups, the ideas of right and wrong behavior (or ethics) of others may be untenable.

In studying the values most commonly designated as part of a social worker's basic guiding commitment, an attempt was made to see what members of the profession described as an ideal way of life. The most helpful guide was to see what changes social workers

6 See Appendix for list of terms used in audited classes, faculty evaluations, and social work literature.
7 See Appendix E, Classified Bibliography (Descriptions of Social Work Values and Ethics).

advocated, as expressed in classes, faculty seminars, and literature, and what things they tried to preserve or defend from change. Historically, and in current professional activity, codes of the ethical norms of social work appear to the author to have been derived from its values rather than the contrary. Social work values have emerged from the experiences of practitioners with what works successfully in a culture oriented ethically as ours is.

VALUES AT VARYING LEVELS OF ABSTRACTION

Philosophers have pointed out two general types of values—abstract concepts of what ought or should be, or ultimate values, and ideas concerning means to achieve those values, often referred to as instrumental values.

The questionnaires seemed to indicate that a majority of teachers use the term "value" in the sense of "ultimate" value, or ideal state, when discussing values as such. In class audits it was clear that the profession has a wide range of operational values, and proximate or immediate goals looking toward ultimate values. Students in the classes observed seemed to become confused when ultimate values were presented abstractly, one by one. When illuminated by specific operational values and illustrated by several reality applications, the nature of the ultimate value as social work conceives it took form.

Since our ultimate values are expressed in terms shared by other professions and popularly used with many meanings, the author wonders if perhaps sound professional education may not require that each value be seen at all levels of abstractions if it is to have usefulness in determining the quality of practice.

When an ultimate value was illustrated in terms of an instrumental value related to social work skill, couched in language with operational meaning, students were able to identify it in practice and use it as a basis for governing their own behavior in the next situation. According to field reports, they had great difficulty in applying ultimate values directly to practice without intermediary steps in conceptualization. Value teaching seemed a thing apart from performance, even though they believed themselves thoroughly in accord with what was presented. For example "respect for the dignity of each individual" was commonly affirmed but students expressed bewilderment as to how one showed "respect." When one teacher related the instrumental value of "confidentiality of disclosures made in the professional relationship" to "respect," a lively class discussion followed. "Confidentiality" or "professional secret" was a value mentioned in every listing of ethical norms. It seems to be more cherished than almost any other single instrumental value, and part of this high regard appears to derive from its universality in application in all social work methods, and from the fact that it is a term used by social work more commonly than by other professions, and hence less easily confused with other professional meanings. It is related to all social work's ultimate values. "Privileged communication" is the more usual legal and cultural expression of the idea. When "confidentiality," in turn, was discussed in relation to "how" it "should" be applied, with illustrations of borderline cases where revelations "might" be "justified," its use as an ethical principle or instrumental means of attaining ultimate values became clear.

This leads to the question as to whether, as time goes on, social work will discover its own terms to describe its values as they are used in governing professional behavior. It appears professionally sound to link our ultimate goals with those of the humanitarian-democratic aspects of our culture, allying the profession with the social conscience and general concern for human well-being, so that society gradually comes to see the profession as a means toward its ultimate ends. But we need to have more vivid expressions to describe the ways our profession helps achieve them. Imaginative teachers and professional philosophers will have to experiment along this line. Meanwhile it seemed clear that high level abstractions should be used sparingly unless accompanied by ample illustrations in concrete terms.

Learning was speeded when field teachers used conference time to relate long-familiar value phrases to social work's implementation of them. Examples are "equality," "freedom," "personal dignity," "social responsibility," "cooperation." Students who were not particularly inclined to philosophic speculation, or impatient at what seemed to them belabored discussion of the obvious in beginning philosophy, ethics and methods courses were much stimulated in conference discussions of "respect for dignity" as seen in reception office routines, confidentiality, provision of adequate budgets, inviolate keeping of agreements, and so on. Field teachers seemed best able to induce philosophic awareness of ultimate goals as a basis for process, and to help students see process as a tool, thus developing a "professional" instead of "craft" approach to skill.

Several students spoke of the difficulty of seeing how values were applied in what they observed and experienced in their field work. Sometimes recommended procedures and policies seemed to be "the self-evident common sense of the matter, hardly to be called a value," to quote a student interview. Sometimes a policy seemed in direct contradiction to an abstract value they were hearing about in methods or philosophy classes. Examination of such instances and accounts of supervisory experience indicated that most often to the student one value seemed applicable, while to the agency or supervisor another seemed to have bearing, both theoretically affirmed by social work. Statements in *Standards for the Professional Practice of Social Work* point up how such difficulties can come about and the educational risks of considering one value at a time.

> Belief in his right to hold and express his own opinions . . . *so long as* by so doing he does not infringe upon the rights of others.
> Framework of a progressive *yet stable* society.
> . . . to assist persons . . . to attain satisfying relationships . . . in accordance with *their particular* wishes . . . and *in harmony* with those of the community.
> Regard as his primary obligation the welfare of the persons served, *consistent with* the common welfare and *as related* to the agency function.
> Right of persons served to make their own decisions . . . *unless* the agency must act in a protective role. (All italics author's.) [8]

All these qualifications, and many others in this document, show the practical difficulties involved in any abstract delineation of values. The social worker has to learn how to determine when rights of others are threatened, when stability becomes more im-

[8] AASW, *Standards for the Professional Practice of Social Work, op. cit.,* 1–2.

portant than desirable change, when community wishes supersede individual self-determination, when obligation to agency function takes precedence over the welfare of individual clients, when protective role is indicated, and so on.

After compiling many statements of social work values at the abstract level from classes, examination papers, professional books and articles, it seemed clear to the author that the basic problem in formulating professionally shared values and ethical norms stems from social work's historic conflict of interests in the reconciling of responsibilities toward the needs of the individuals immediately served, the needs of closely associated individuals, and the needs of unknown individuals in the total society. In any listing of values which was studied, values concerning the individual, such as acceptance of people regardless of their personal characteristics, might have been placed in parallel position to corresponding values concerning society, such as recognition of and utilization of variety.

Typical teaching today does not always present values in this way, however. Often individual considerations are taken up serially, followed by social considerations. Not always is equal attention given to both, and especially, concrete examples of their interaction are not studied. Students who had from the beginning semester seen "individual need" and "common good" discussed together as inextricably interwoven, appeared, as indicated in field and course reports, to make transfer between abstract principle and practical solution most easily and consistently. As one of the *Ad Hoc* Panel members expressed it, you cannot produce a rule of thumb for the application of ethical judgment based on accepted values; but you can teach how to identify many different considerations that always have a bearing under any conditions.

HIGHLY ABSTRACT VALUES

The "ultimate values" most frequently mentioned in questionnaires, course content, class audits, and professional literature might be summarized as follows: [9]

  1. Each human being should be regarded by all others as an

[9] A compilation of all statements found in the literature (see Appendix E, Classified Bibliography, Descriptions of Social Work Values and Ethics) and statements of goals on the questionnaires. In their present form they are the author's own interpretation of this mass of material, but similar wording was found in numerous places.

object of infinite worth. He should be preserved in a state commensurate with his innate dignity and protected from suffering.

2. Human beings have large and as yet unknown capacities for developing both inner harmony and satisfaction and ability to make outward contributions to the development of others.

3. In order to realize his potentialities every human being must interact in giving and taking relationships with others, and has an equal right to opportunities to do so.

4. Human betterment is possible. Change, growth, movement, progress, improvement are terms appearing constantly in social work value statements, inferring social work's confidence that individually and collectively, human beings have capacity to change. Thus change *per se* is not sought, but change toward personal and social ideals affirmed by the profession, is something "better."

5. Change in a positive direction, for individuals, groups, or organized societies, may be speeded by active and purposive assistance or encouragement from others. Change in a negative direction may be slowed or prevented by the intervention of others. In other words, "helping" is a process of demonstrated validity, and is a value to be respected in its own right.

6. The most effective changes cannot be imposed. Man's potentialities include his capacity to discover and direct his own destiny. This capacity, unless lacking or grossly impaired, must be respected.

7. Much concerning man is knowable. Human effort should be directed to constant search for enlarged understanding of man's needs and potentialities. What already has been discovered should be made available and utilized in devising means to enhance individual and social self-fulfillment.

8. The profession of social work is a group committed to the preservation and implementation of these values.

No two social workers would word statements in exactly the same way; each prefers his particular version. Many other values were mentioned, but these selected appeared in nearly every statement examined, and most other values were related to them.

One of the major philosophic points of discussion going on currently in faculty curriculum planning is whether social work's primary commitment is to the individual or to the good of the whole society. It is this author's personal opinion that the two cannot be separated and must be seen constantly together as a field of interaction. Therefore it seems possible that if many of social work's expressed values could be paired or grouped and taught as aspects of ultimate values, conflicts between the individual and others would be minimized and the student would gradually develop an intellectual habit of thinking of *both*. Social work's concepts of the interrelatedness and wholeness of man would be emphasized. For instance:

Importance of the individual	⟷ Interdependence of all individuals at all times
Consideration for and acceptance of differences	⟷ Social utilization of and provisions for variability within flexible expectations
Self-determination Right to select own life-style	⟷ Consideration for self-determining needs and desires of others
Self-help	⟷ Obligation to assist others in developing or recovering this capacity; non-blaming acceptance when self-help is not possible
Common needs of man	⟷ Recognition of similarities as well as differences
Acceptance of every *person*	⟷ No condoning of *behavior* which hurts others
Right to equal participation	⟷ Granting participation to others
Right to protection of body and intellect	⟷ Obligation not to injure or deprive others
Freedom	⟷ Limits
Change—Progress—Growth	⟷ Preservation of the effective; stability; security; social direction through accepted norms
Validated knowledge	⟷ Intuitive speculation; insight

Students would have to be shown that such a scheme is suggestive, not rigid in nature, and has final validity only at the operational level.

MIDDLE RANGE ABSTRACTIONS OF IDEALS

In order to achieve these values, social work has used scientific and philosophic understandings and seems to have fairly well delineated some ideals which have taken on meaning as values to be striven for in accord with these ultimate values. Often they are regarded as proximate or intermediary goals. Some of the following phrases were used in class teaching:

1. The well-functioning person: A more detailed description would be developed in the Curriculum Study's projects on Human Growth and Behavior and on the Social Work Methods. Perceptive of outer and inner forces; aware of own limitations and abilities; ability to value self and others; ability to utilize opportunities he finds in society and to adjust to limitations; ability to meet social role requirements.

2. The good family: Provides for physical, emotional, spiritual, intellectual nurture; sensitive to varying needs of each member at each stage of ego development; grants each member participation in decision-making; accepts and adapts to limitations of each member while striving to overcome or lessen them.

3. The growth-enhancing group: Sees needs of each member; opportunity for participation at many levels; develops own objectives and ways of achieving them.

4. The good community: Provides institutional means for realizing desires of members; provides machinery for determining member desires; provides avenue of usefulness for minorities.

The class response to such concepts made the author question whether we do not often look at the wrong level of abstraction to find social work's most characteristic values and unique contribution to the formulation of goals for mankind. Each of these main areas of professional interest and knowledge contains ideas borrowed from social science, medicine or politics, but there seemed to be a fusion of such materials into unitary concepts at this level which is not as yet described in much of the literature, although unmistakably real and vital in the teaching process observed.

Fragmentary accounts in field supervisors' reports strengthened this hypothesis and were the only source of practice observation available for examination in this study. The few processed records of supervision available corroborated the conviction of those who believe study of the use of values in practice must precede complete formulation of content objectives.[10] If the work of inexperienced beginners, feeling their way, yields such suggestive material, analysis of mature practice where what is in the mind of the worker is frankly and candidly described would probably be much more rewarding.

It is interesting to note in passing that one teacher, whose class almost breathlessly had followed an analysis of a record, apologized afterward to the author for having "touched on no values at all" during the session. Yet forty-six specific statements had been tabulated by the author, all having to do with explicit aims as to what was being hoped for in a group process, both for individuals and the combination of members. Twenty-one additional goals, or disvalues to be overcome, seemed to be assumed or taken for granted, though identification of these wholly depended on the author's impression of the sense of the discussion. The teacher, when questioned a bit, explained she had in mind discussion of such subjects as "worth," "democracy," "self-determination." All of these, in the author's opinion, had been covered in some form, but at the level of abstraction where they are lived out as immediate tasks to be accomplished, if possible.

In classes where it was possible to audit before the exact purpose of the author's visit was known and had made the teacher self-conscious, the constant use of middle range abstractions was even more apparent—descriptions of what social work hopes can be realized for *any* person, family, school, group, community, etc. Usually these were given as background for understanding a specific situation, but not always. When presented as organized theory, it gave the author the impression that potentially we are on the verge of a rich literature, and that theorists in the profession might well give attention to this aspect of possible professional knowledge, to move it from an assumed to a more clearly defined area of content.

[10] *Cf.* Chapter I, Issue #1.

Much the same might be said of ethical behavior in social workers. Another teacher commented she had intended to "pull out all stops" with respect to use of the *Standards for the Professional Practice of Social Work* but had not found the tenor of class discussion conducive. Yet she used the word "should" eleven times and said "the worker is absolutely obligated to" at one point, each item having its counterpart in the document. One might question whether social workers and social work educators have a clear sense of what a "value" really is as a vital part of practice theory and technique, and also whether "good practice" has been presented to students as a consistently "ethical" procedure. This schism between our theoretic models and our technical formulation of goals for individual case or group situation must somehow be bridged.

A cumulative impression gained through talks with teachers and class audits surprised the author. There seemed to be a core body of accepted goals, regardless of auspices, professional specialty, or personal experiences of the teachers. Each teacher or school, no doubt, had his own "plus" to add from his cultural and philosophic orientation, but a base of agreement seemed apparent. Nowhere was this more clearly brought to the project director's attention than in discussions of the "good family," a topic where traditionally personal orientations have often been thought to cause wide philosophic divergence. For example, a teacher in a publicly financed school discussed the importance of providing for changing growth and needs and emotional balance between family members, in almost exactly the same phraseology as that used in one of the sectarian schools, and paralleled statements not quite as exact in quotation were found in two others. One wonders whether commonality within the profession will not first be clarified at this middle level of abstraction and formulated into an irreducible kernel of professional value orientation.

INSTRUMENTAL VALUES

As one proceeds to instrumental values, wider divergence of opinions occurs; interpretation becomes more difficult. Actual situations are extremely important to use as illustrations and much teaching becomes an examination of alternatives. For example, such questions rise as "Is a 'good' family ever a divorced family?"

"Does a 'good' government prevent bloodshed at the cost of individual social participation?" "Does a 'good' court always have to take account of religious preferences in foster care placement?"

Whatever divergencies there may be at this level, some commonly accepted instrumental values seem to emerge in frequent references in both class and field instruction, such as:

1. The "good" social agency: Mediates between individual needs and community impulses to help; respects the competence of each employee; provides physical, intellectual, organizational atmosphere conducive to exercise of competence; adapts to changing individual and community needs.

2. The "good" government: Provides stable setting for individual and community growth; allows for equal participation of members; provides means for altering its own decisions.

3. The "good" professional person: Takes form as a value ideal of high instrumental significance. Most of the following components of the ideal professional self were assembled from statements in class audits or student evaluations, a few came from questionnaires.

Obligation always to seek a whole view of man—his physical, feeling, thinking, sensing attributes; refusal to consider any single aspect of man exclusive of regard for the others.

Respect for the nature of responsibilities involved in professional relation to others. Relationship is seen as a powerful force whose use must be safeguarded and always directed to the interests of the helped. "The relationship" has become an instrumental value.

Awareness of the characteristics of the worker's self as an instrument.

Ability to work with all kinds of people. (This was listed most frequently in evaluations.)

A non-blaming, non-exhorting, warm, receptive approach to people. (Other phrases used were non-judgmental, non-moralistic, educational rather than directing, non-punitive.)

Acceptance of persons, groups and communities as they are; interest shown in their past or current behavior and life patterns only as it is to be utilized in helping them.

Perception of himself as a communicator of values, preserver of values, and "norm-bender" or changer of values.

THE ETHICS OF THE PROFESSION

Judging from statements of teachers to their classes, the profession seems to have developed many more tacitly understood or unwritten conceptions of what a social worker "ought," "should," "is obligated," "is bound" to do than have been codified. The new worker should be familiar with historic and current attempts to reach professional consensus. The difficulty in making a theoretic or generalized approach operationally valid and useful was revealed in responses to the questionnaire. The problems from practice presented for response followed as closely as possible items in *Standards for the Professional Practice of Social Work*. The fact that very few of those answering mentioned the code, and that answers were so varied it was impossible to categorize them in systematic order, suggests that when considering specific alternatives of professional behavior the profession does not yet think in terms of a code of ethics. A number of respondents said in effect, "It would depend on the situation, enough details of which were not furnished."

Yet students clamor for, and are perhaps justified in wanting, guiding principles and some generalized approaches. Like the values, in order to become real, each ethical suggestion should be accompanied by both negative and positive illustrations from a variety of settings; when observed and when not observed. Particularly, illustrations of qualifying conditions are needed, such as when self-determination must be limited in the interest of others; when a worker may be justified in continuing with an agency which does not observe the code; when client interest must give way to group or community interest. Again, by teaching both considerations at the same time, a sense of how ethical judgment is exercised may be communicated.[11] Ethics can best be comprehended when all possible actions and considerations are reviewed, and the consequences of like action in the past are evaluated. If the consequences are likely to violate a fundamental value, then ethically the social worker "ought not" to follow that bit of behavior.

[11] An explanation of such an approach is described in Ian McGreal, *The Art of Making Choices* (Dallas: Southern Methodist Press, 1953).

Except for the presentation of published codes, the separation of "how" ethics are taught from "what" is taught seemed even more difficult than with values. The process of teaching was, therefore, examined in some detail, as illustrative material from field reports and classroom occurrences were assembled. By far the most illustrations came from accounts of field experiences; and suggested the kind of content that has to be provided in some form. Whether all of this content is most suitably left to field instruction is another matter which can be determined only in the consideration of each individual curriculum. The following data indicate the nature of the content in field instruction and also in other courses.

FIELD INSTRUCTION

One classroom teacher suggested in her reply to the questionnaire that professional ethics for the caseworker was "just good casework." Field instructors can do much to show how the "best service possible" is the basis of professional ethics, and at the same time show how professional performance involves assurance that due consideration will be given to the weighing of many factors which always need to be considered and which have been identified as characteristic professional concerns. Ethics taught as a distillation of professional experience, classified into typical situations repeatedly confronted, helped students develop integrity and consistency in their professional behavior. Supervisory recognition of a specific practice decision or bit of worker behavior as an exemplification of what the profession has defined as desirable, uniformly seemed to give students a feeling of satisfaction in identifying themselves as professional persons and stimulated deeper commitment to whatever value or principle was involved.

Calling attention to aspects of agency structure which illustrated personnel standards or conformed to civil rights principles similarly helped students to see their agency as part of the professional stream, and to perceive social work as a profession developing standards which can be put into operation. The difference in norms of ordinary social usage and professional behavior have to be distinguished. A student regretted having revealed that his own family came from the same geographic area as a client. This was utilized in field teaching to show "that becoming personal is contraindicated because it tends to interfere with the worker's helpfulness." The supervisor found this experience helped the student understand the need for a professional self.

Helping the student distinguish between clients' aspirations and his own was an indispensable part of field teaching in all methods. One student for example, was anxious to help a group become interested in redecorating their meeting place which seemed drab to him. The supervisor helped him discover it was clean and attractive to group members. A husband's behavior seemed brusque and neglectful to the student, but followed a nationality pattern of detached aloofness on the part of the family head and was highly satisfying to the wife as evidence of the man's possessive feeling toward his home.

Acquiring a professional value as part of the self comes in learning to distinguish which standards of behavior may be a matter of custom or individual preference and which are viewed as operationally essential to personality growth as the profession conceives it. The same student who learned to recognize and accept how the wife felt about husbandly norms was helped to see that in another case his personal reaction that physical abuse of a child could not be tolerated was sound. Such behavior was irreconcilable with goals for release of every child's inner resentments and ultimate growth, even though culturally these parents felt that they had unlimited rights to authoritarian handling of their children.

In teaching the use of limits with clients and groups, demonstrating of the social worker's scrupulous regard for them was presented as one use of self in helping. Accounting for money entrusted to a group, apology for accidental roughness, care not to encroach on private property, were bits of personal ethical behavior which received teacher approval as use of personal values to help. Client interest in sex or family mores of the worker can be often interpreted as client effort to make use of relationship. "Do you try to get home on time for supper?" was a question avoided by a student. His supervisor helped him later experiment with acting out his behavior in this regard so that an immature young husband sensed the worker's personal integrity in practicing what he was trying to develop with respect to family responsibility. A group worker refused to be party to plans for inducting a professional athlete as a team member in order to win a close contest. When the group directly questioned whether this was an agency rule or personal standard, the student worker was able to show it was both, that he agreed with and himself practiced agency norms on eligibility.

Field work gives constant chance for practice of all the ethical and value implications in perception of role and status and identification with agency as a social force designed to facilitate change and growth. One illustration was that of a student to whom the requirement of client accountability in the use of money seemed a violation of his belief in acceptance and trust in people's ability to handle their own affairs. He was helped to see that expectations of meeting requirements of responsibility do not conflict with expectations of ability.

One of the most puzzling problems, mentioned repeatedly in discussion of field learning, was how to handle the observations of astute students who discover discrepancies between the ideals and behavior norms of the profession as they are presented in classes, literature and codes, and the policies and everyday practice of agencies and staff members. Some of the agency situations students most often mentioned to supervisors and faculty advisors as conflicts were:

Failure to meet need on the minimum adequate basis described in classes as essential.

Exclusion policies regarding acceptance of clients for service. These included sectarian or racial restrictions, social class restrictions on boards, economic restrictions through fee charging.

Agency failure to participate in social action campaigns related to problems met by its clientele.

Punitive practices in other departments of agency activities (especially true in mental hospitals and prisons).

Policy influence of persons in the economic or political power structure which outweighed other group opinions, clients', popular, or social work professional.

Seeming manipulation of individuals and groups to induce a preconceived pattern of performance. Students often perceived offering the client choices between alternatives as actually somehow weighting the advantages of one.

Students who had least confusion over such discrepancies were those who had been taught ultimate values along with the concept that their attainment through proximate goals would be slow and partial. In instances where agency performance did not meet all prescribed professional standards, a frank recognition of agency limitations and hopes to correct the difficulty was a helpful learning experience. In a term paper a fourth semester student criticized a supervisor's attempt to explain sectarian practice as giving reasons that were rationalizations. The student believed he could work within the restriction, but saw himself trying, after graduation and more experience, to work for policies that would not limit clientele, regardless of sponsorship. He could not see himself defending sectarian restrictions as desirable indefinitely.

Nothing seemed to reassure students and speed their learning more than discovery that agency and supervisor activity was directed toward eventual correction of what some students talked about as "the gap" (between ideals and actuality). When the supervisor utilized historical perspective to compare present allowances with former ones, the present amount of unsegregated social work with that of a past period, etc. students were helped to identify with "agency" as a means of achieving values. If, as a number of writers believe,[12] one of the most trying demands of the profession is to live with the constant frustration that the individual social worker is often helpless to effect changes he sees as desirable, some practice in how to deal with such discrepancies and yet maintain personal and professional integrity is a highly important part of field learning. Use of professional channels for correcting inconsistencies is especially helpful. Students participated in preparing material to stimulate interest in higher allowances, defend civil rights, watched appeals for personnel changes. One student was able directly to make suggestions for working out the use of an agency resource on a racially unsegregated basis.

COURSES IN CASEWORK

Casework courses offer continuous opportunity to point out the operation of professional ethics. These phrases occurred in audits: "The worker is *obligated* to refer a client with medical symptoms

12 *E.g.*, Babcock, *op. cit.*

to a physician and *must not* assume psychosomatic illness." "One *must* consider how the younger children are going to be affected by the worker's concentration on [oldest]." "The worker *should have* explained she could not share information secured from a client." "*Should* the father have been seen as well as the mother?" "*Must* we withhold information [from a cooperating agency] which might make treatment more effective?" Teachers helped students generalize from such incidents and provided meaning to the code of ethics by referring to passages where general approaches to typical choices are considered. One student impulsively verbalized his relief by commenting, "I'm tired of hearing 'It all depends on the situation.' I've been in school long enough to know that. What I *need* to know is some way *always* to look at every situation, and make sure I'm considering everything I should."

Two ethical principles for which casework methods courses are certain to have illustrative material are the confidential nature of disclosures and the obligation to follow the policies and carry out the function of the employing agency. Social work's patterns of communication with colleagues and cooperating agencies, the "professional manners" of social work, are almost inevitably illustrated.

Another aspect of the use of values in practice according to ethical standards seems not to be stressed in the professional literature on casework but frequently was raised in student papers and field practice. This is the worker's use of his own value system in helping the client determine his. With habitual law breakers, acting-out adolescents, and others whose behavior deviates widely from usual community norms, the question of how the worker accepts the person without condoning his behavior constantly comes up. Students wonder "what to say" when asked directly how they would behave, etc.

An illustration of such a situation is found in "The Unmarried Mother's Search for Standards," as follows:

> The worker remarked that Martha had a right to be cross. Apparently she had given M. the idea that she did not feel there should be limits, but this was not so . . .
>
> Martha probably wanted to know whether the worker did the things young people do and really approved of the things about

which she appeared tolerant. *She assured Martha that she did.*
(Italics author's.) [13]

Two students commented that they found descriptions of worker
approach, manner, vocabulary helpful and wished the social
worker as well as client might be described. Descriptions might not
really satisfy or provide good learning content, but more detailed
accounts like the interaction above appear to be needed.

COURSES IN GROUP WORK

In audits of classes and in student evaluations more questions arose
in the group work courses than in any other sequence concerning
the ethical behavior of the social worker and problems of value
conflicts. Group work students also contributed productively in
classes on generic method and human behavior and social services
informational courses. They were a source of stimulus to other
class members in their thinking along broadly philosophic lines.
This seemed to be more than an accidental occurrence due to the
small number of classes audited. The group worker is immediately
brought face to face with the underlying ethical problem in social
work—the root philosophic question with which social work has
always struggled: shall individual or social "good" be the final
criterion by which to measure any proposed action?

The group worker deals with society in microcosm and the beginning worker at once senses numerous forces are at play and
becomes part of them in a way that cannot be ignored. Technical
skill and knowledge and a working philosophic approach are at
once required for taking account of social processes as well as
internal individual personality formation.

Some of the questions demanding orientation to values, which
group workers had to face and which were brought up in class
were:

[13] Jane K. Goldsmith, "The Unmarried Mother's Search for Standards," *Social Case
work*, XXXVIII, 2 (February, 1957), 73. Sylvan S. Furman (ed.), *Reaching the Unreached* (2nd ed.; New York: New York City Youth Board, 1954), Sol Wiener Ginsburg, "The Impact of the Social Worker's Cultural Structure on Social Therapy,"
Social Casework, XXXII, 8 (October, 1951), 319–325, and Bertram Beck, "The Exile
of Those in Conflict with the Law," in *Casework Papers, 1955*, from the National
Conference of Social Work (New York: Family Service Association of America, 1955),
32–42, also take up the problem of how much the worker should divulge of his own
value system.

How far can deviant behavior be tolerated, even if positively purposive and perhaps a mark of progress for the individual (*e.g.,*
exaggerated aggressions in a hitherto withdrawn member), if it
interferes with attaining group goals?

How much can one precipitate an individual's awareness of his own
limitations and deviations from accepted norms? Is the social worker's responsibility to help him find help or not to interfere except
at his request?

Can self-determination be permitted to threaten agency standing
with its board or community?

How does one show acceptance of cultural patterns contrary to the
worker's personal standards or the agency's values (*e.g.,* sectarian
differences)?

What is the essence of "democracy?" How help carry out majority
determination and also respect the minority? How deal with an
authoritarian natural leader to whom the group submits even
though individually they disapprove of him? How handle group
determined plans contrary to usual or "acceptable" social standards in our culture?

How much to encourage change in group members which is contrary to family, neighborhood, cultural group patterns?

What use should be made of confidential disclosures about anti-social
activities?

How much should workers encourage social action to correct inequities which may cast the group or its members in unfavorable light
in their natural groupings?

How does one convey the idea of "limits" in individual behavior
and group activity?

Whose values does the worker represent—community's, agency's, or
his own?

Group workers faced immediate conflicts between "acceptance,"
a "non-judgmental" approach, "beginning where the client is,"
and the awareness that group work agencies are culture bearers to
which the community has assigned responsibility for preserving
and enforcing many social norms. This conflict was usually pre-
cipiated earlier than in casework student experience. Caseworkers
were either assigned initial cases where client behavior was not
grossly anti-social (*e.g.,* old age assistance) or were in agencies designed to tolerate extreme behavior deviations (as in a mental

hospital). Permissiveness did not so immediately react on other persons equally deserving the worker's attention.

The group work situation lends itself to teaching values in constellations or choices and balance between opposites—permissiveness and freedom of choice within prescribed limits; democratic determination of goals by the group and injection of authority, and so on.

COURSES IN COMMUNITY ORGANIZATION

The ethical problem of how to stand firm on goals a professional social worker considers of paramount importance and at the same time to "start where the client (community) is" was brought out many times in courses audited and in assignments found in course outlines. The hairline difference had constantly to be drawn between effecting a workable compromise accepting agency and cultural limitations, and rationalizing or capitulating to the status quo.

Community organization methods courses provided concrete illustrations of how culturally conditioned atitudes affect the status of social workers and the possibilities of improvement in the life experiences of their clients. "Rugged individualism," partisan, religious, and class bias, social responsibility for defining minimum standards of meeting need, the use of punishment versus rehabilitation were some of the problems presented which involved weighing of values. Practice in the recognition of the underlying assumptions around which intergroup conflicts occur was possible in every record examined by class groups.

The contribution which practicing social workers in agencies can make toward elimination of injustices and the enhancement of dignified living conditions for many persons was a positive learning experience for many students, which appeared to be particularly valuable when given in the second or third semester. It offset the feeling that the worker in an individual job touched the lives of few people, and helped students discover effective professional outlets for idealistic goals they brought to social work. The concept that every social worker has a professional as well as citizen responsibility to help correct conditions affecting potential as well as actual clientele was reassuring and a help in gaining an integrated picture of social work goals. More than in any other place in the curriculum the social process involved, from detection and measurement of need to social provision and final use of provided resources, was made vivid. Students saw themselves a part of the process, and social work as a functional part of society as a whole.

COURSES IN RESEARCH

The research courses, including the project, yielded many possibilities for the growth of ethical judgment and a deeper understanding of social work's value commitments. The relation between value judgments and empirically validated criteria had to be dealt with. Research courses made clear that many of social work's assumptions and standards have not been scientifically verified and perhaps cannot be measured in an absolute sense for many years, if ever. For example, one class endeavoring to develop a system for classifying foster homes discovered the difficulties of weighing a "good" foster home when a practical decision had to be made between the advantages of a single bed or the presence of a potential sibling. Data reported to this study showed that research courses helped students learn (1) to recognize value judgments as such, (2) to see them as not necessarily "unwarranted" or "unscientific" but as part of the framework of social work, and (3) to realize that as such they constitute data that must be assessed before any measurement can proceed.

The ethics of experimentation was a subject with which students had a good deal of trouble. When the basic methods courses stressed the need of scientific examination and showed uses made of experimentally discovered knowledge, research teachers were able to discuss safeguards in the experimental use of clients without negative student reaction. Control groups, trying out new techniques, use of confidentially disclosed information as data, the dangers of setting up a study to prove rather than to test usefulness of present hypotheses about people, are some of the aspects of research which sometimes seemed to conflict with other social work values. The social work goal of helping the individual or society to change took on enlarged meaning for many students when confronted with the need to assess what is change and what changes are "better." Theses frequently offered opportunity to weigh some of social work's values. The great contribution of the research sequence to the learning of values and ethics appeared to be helping students integrate the two values of scientific validation and artistic use of sensitivity and insight. In showing the relation between assumptions based on belief, hunch, or casual experience, and present or experimental technical procedures, students were helped to discover another professional channel through which their idealistic aspirations and philosophic doubts might be resolved—systematic research.

COURSES IN ADMINISTRATION

Courses discussed with teachers and written accounts of episodes in class discussion indicated a wide difference in the way values are currently handled in administration courses. They revealed much opportunity to show how community aspirations are achieved through effective agency machinery, a chance to see "agency" as an orderly means of securing desirable objectives at the least social cost. One student designated administration as the course he believed had contributed most to his understanding of professional ethics and values.

The ethics of the professional worker's attitude toward policy already formulated and responsibility for contributing to policy formation as means to desirable ends can be presented as real situations in these courses. Such courses seemed to be a logical and effective place for teaching standards as to a "good" agency, and mutual or interlocking obligations of agency and worker. The profession as work was often stressed, and its functional contribution in society. Students questioned the ethics of management skills as being a form of manipulation of people. "Lines of authority" concepts were looked at as positive ways of achieving the end or value of service, and also as possible rationalizations of authoritarian motivation and personal desires for power. Observations in the scope of this study were much too sketchy to be more than possibly suggestive, but it appeared that when administrative techniques were immediately illustrated by their ultimate effect on the service received by people, students were helped to see efficiency and administrative process as instrumental values. When presented theoretically as a mechanism or system, negative personal feelings concerning relation to authority were reinforced. Student comments on administration courses were more confused and mixed than about any other courses in the curriculum.

CONCLUSIONS

As in values, most social work ethical confrontations involve judgment concerning professional obligations to the persons to be served, and to others. Problems of self-interest, agency interest, and professional interest are associated with efforts to determine priorities in obligation.

Values and ethics of the social work profession are not unique and its goals and concerns have to be presented as related to the goals and concerns of other professions. Any uniqueness in social work appears to stem from an implicit commitment to relate to both individual and general good. For example, in a number of class sessions it was explicitly stated that a doctor or nurse had little cause to feel obligated to persons not directly receiving service; the social worker on the other hand was obligated to include them in all considerations.

To the author, it therefore follows that the social work value system may most effectively be presented in teaching as a series of constellations which take account of ideals for each individual and of all of society at the same time in one large interacting field of concern.

Ethics in our profession are primarily focused on how to balance the two.

CHAPTER IV

The Nature of the Learning Process with Respect to Values

The chief source of data regarding the learner of values and ethics was the permanent records of student progress as seen in supervisors' reports of field instruction and final evaluations. Such records were suggested by faculty members of assisting schools for two groups of students, superior ones and those whose work was marginal. (See Chapter II, page 34.) These were all students who in the usual selection process had been adjudged persons who had good potentiality for becoming effective practicing social workers.

Although not selected by highly scientific means the records did, in fact, include students from a wide variety of backgrounds with respect to race, national heritage, section of the country, size of home community, religious affiliation and parental occupational and economic status. Application procedure varied to such an extent that complete and comparable data on these items were not available on all, but there appeared to be no outstanding difference between "good" and "poor" students in these respects.

PREPARATION AND READINESS TO LEARN

There was not sufficient uniformity of information nor large enough groupings to do a statistical compilation, but an apparent difference did emerge between the two groups of students with respect to one factor in application material, which was found in the records reviewed in all eight schools.

The highly successful students expressed themselves definitely at time of application regarding values they cherished most highly. Regarding religion, for example, as a group they had a settled notion (pro or con) regarding humanism, supernatural beliefs, religious authority, and so on. In nearly every "good" student, a fairly well formed philosophy of life and beliefs concerning desirable personal behavior *for himself* seemed to have developed with a feeling of commitment and obligation to it. However, in a number of the most successful students, it was also apparent that they already had developed and could articulate a willingness for others to have different values, and had some sense that with respect to their own values, there were different ways of interpreting what kind of behavior best exemplified them. They did not express a desire to teach, evangelize, or impose their ideas on others. Their idea of what helping might be seemed to center on making the other person more comfortable from his point of view rather than persuading him to follow their own pattern of life. They were much concerned with changing social conditions to insure greater equality. Their urge seemed to be to expand tolerance of variation. There was willingness to believe that change in social conditions and personal behavior was apt to be partial and slow.

In contrast, application statements of the poorer students showed that they seemed less articulate about their own values. They expressed desire to help by teaching some "better way" which they could describe only in terms of their own values. The urge to change people was expressed frequently in terms of how they might be helped to achieve certain patterns of life. They were more concerned with changing individuals and spoke less often of changing social conditions.

From this extremely fragmentary descriptive material, adherence to some definite philosophic position would seem to have been an indication for success, providing the prospective student did not feel compelled to force others to it.

In the learning process the most successful students did not reject the value system they came with, but changed with respect to their conception of its application in human situations. They seemed to see the "social work approach" as an expansion or illumination of the underlying intent and meaning of values they had already learned to accept. Interviews with first year students tended to confirm this. They felt a deep desire to avoid applying their own standards to others, but found their standards reinforced and confirmed by social work experience. In a sectarian school, a student stopped the project director after a class audit to say, "I used to take my values as a matter of course—something you could do automatically. Now I know what charity and the brotherhood of man could mean if we only knew more about how to be *really* charitable." When pressed for a bit of the sense of what "being charitable" now meant to him, he said "It means you want to like them no matter what they think nor how many mistakes they make, not just that you act as though you liked them. You'd like to see them leading the good life but you know they must decide that and can't be made to."

In a non-sectarian school a second semester student expressed astonishment at the change in himself, but thought he had not changed any of the basic beliefs or goals for people he had when he came. The main change he saw was "good things cannot be taken for granted. There are lots of good ways of getting to the same goal. I used to believe in just a few." Student progress seemed to hinge on learning how to handle that part of their own personalities which involved ideas of right and wrong, in the many relationships occurring in professional performance—with clients, colleagues, and the general public.

An attempt was made to note from student records what philosophy or ethics courses these students had had at undergraduate level. It appeared that only about half had had any such courses, though titles and course numbers often did not indicate course content and no exact estimation was possible. A good many had had sociology or political science, which presumably might contain such material. More "good" students than "poor" ones had had some type of course that might be construed as dealing with philosophic alternatives, but the small numbers involved made the significance of such a difference doubtful.

The author gained an impression, however, that it would be unwise to assume that students entering the Master's program have even a rudimentary notion of how to think philosophically regarding such concepts as common versus individual good; proximate versus ultimate goals; the nature of "the right;" the meaning of value, choice, responsibility, duty, authority, and human rights. Previous grappling with such classic philosophic questions might help orient students to thinking about social work values and ethics, but gearing graduate ethics or philosophy courses to pre-supposed or assumed standard philosophic understandings would seem educationally risky. As might have been anticipated, in the sectarian schools a higher proportion of students than in others had taken philosophy, and a good share of their student bodies was familiar with the common over-all philosophic framework, so that somewhat more could be taken for granted as a common starting point than in schools drawing their students from less homogeneous backgrounds. Nevertheless, their faculties described almost exactly the same problem in helping students learn to use their established value ideas in solving social work problem situations as did the faculties of other schools. Problems regarding "self-determination," "professional judgment," "democracy," "equal participation re-gardless of personal characteristics," "deviant behavior," "fixed standards," occurred in all schools with no apparent relation to auspice or type of student body. This means that methods and social work philosophy and ethics teachers may have to be prepared to introduce some of these concepts *as such* before social work adaptations of them can become clear.

STAGES IN LEARNING

Analysis of the learning process as it pertained to values and ethics revealed three rather distinct stages in most of the student records: an orientation period during which an enthusiastic reaction to the "social work culture" was particularly marked; a period of ques-tioning and disillusionment regarding the validity and applica-bility of professional values; a period of panic and fear regarding the students' own professional competence for implementing values. These seemingly characteristic stages were discussed in group meetings of faculty at several of the assisting schools and with the panel. Opinion was expressed that this impression of the author coincided with the observations of teachers and field super-visors; these periods usually do occur and are part of a typical learning process, although they merge with one another and differ in length and intensity with each student.

The panel felt it would be useful to bear these stages in mind when constructing a curriculum or devising learning experiences. Much more material came to light in student evaluations, student interviews, and faculty suggestions concerning the orientation period than the other stages. This was true partly because the impact of the social work cultural milieu was involved, which, of course, is a continuing influence throughout the school experience. The significant elements in the professional culture stood out most clearly in beginning weeks; both students and faculty recalled that period most vividly. If a foundation were not laid in those early weeks, it appeared that the entire learning process often was slowed or partially ineffective.

THE ORIENTATION PERIOD: INITIATION IN THE PROFESSIONAL CULTURE

Students arrive with the desire to succeed and enthusiasm about becoming "professional." They anxiously seize on externals which appear to them to be characteristic professional behaviors. In their confusion they do not "hear" with total understanding, but this initial eagerness often can be capitalized and made into a firm beginning professional identification. Here social science information concerning how a person learns when coming from one culture into another might be of use.[1] Although acquiring a professional subculture may be a much less intensive change than moving into a totally new culture, we may need to learn more about such processes.It was in this problem, that the inability to distinguish between *what* values are learned and *how* they are learned was most apparent. The exact content of the learning which accrues by simply being one of the actors in a dynamic, interacting association of people is hard to define and assess as to its significant lasting influence. The following aspects of the cultural impact of social work stood out most clearly, and appear to be in line with social science speculation about the acquisition of new cultural patterns. These culture-contact phenomena appeared to this author to be highly effective contributing factors in the development of behavior suited to the demands of professional performance.

[1] For example, Kluckhohn and Murray, "Personality Formation, the Determinants," in *Personality in Nature, Society, and Culture, op. cit.;* Lewin, *op. cit.;* Robin M. Williams, Jr., "Religion, Value Orientations, and Intergroup Conflict," *Journal of Social Issues,* XII, 3 (1956), 12–20.

1. *Identification with the Many-sided Interests of Prominent or Highly Successful Practitioners.*

It has been established that much is learned by copying personal ideals—"the head man"—"the success." Students identify teachers as "good" social workers, but also learn from seeing social workers who are not teachers in either classroom or field. Students speak of noticing distinguished executives, other high-ranking staff members, workers in other agencies. At this beginning point, a number of students told of finding value in professional meetings, not so much for the content of discussion as for the feeling it gave concerning the way in which professional people referred to clients and colleagues, the undefined assumptions that they took for granted in discussing common problems. In the classroom they express interest in social workers of the past, in knowing who prominent social workers of the present are; they are interested in what journals are professionally authoritative.

During this period it might be considered whether it is best to trust less to chance and more formally to insure that students see a variety of social workers in action. There was some indication that supervisors and executives, out of modesty or the desire to keep interpersonal relationships strictly professional, withhold information or neglect to tell about their own activities. The effort to focus solely on the activities of the learner is at times educationally sound, but raises the question whether it satisfies the need of the student for a larger identification than with just those persons who help with his own problems of practice.

For instance a student, later rated as very successful, stalled at a very common philosophic learning block—whether all that social workers do is to help members of the group conform to and accept questionable environmental and social norm requirements, when their non-conformity largely springs from the fact that the society was not meeting their basic needs. A big point in his early learning came when he found the assistant executive of the agency had been actively working for better public housing in the neighborhood even though public housing was disapproved by many of the members of the board of the agency. The supervisor arranged for the student group to hear more about this. The executive was very reluctant at first, but the result was that the entire student group took an immediate greater interest in the individuals in their own groups, and in learning technical skill. Discovering that the professional person had ways of dealing with the conditions which had left them feeling helpless acted as a spur rather than a means of escape from technical problems.

The author's observations would lead to the conclusion that early planned experience which gives the student a feeling that there is breadth as well as intensity in professional concerns is essential and could be used more generally than at present. The outside activities of the superivsor probably may mean most—a feeling that he regards such concerns as a vital part of his job. Intellectualizing on the possibility of doing this in supervisory conferences means less than knowledge of the actual doing.

Students more often knew about outside activities of faculty members, but here, too, conscious effort to share experiences, such as taking part in legislative hearings, writing effective interpretative publicity, and working with organizations promoting increased educational, health, and social opportunities, yielded rich learning dividends.

While students gained much from seeing social workers taking part in all professional concerns, they also needed early reassurance that the executive personnel was interested in the progress of the individuals, neighborhoods, groups and families that were the immediate practice responsibility of workers, as well as in the prestige and efficiency of the agency. In large agencies and schools, there seemed to be real danger that too early emphasis on procedural form, before its utility in serving the helping and learning processes was clear in terms of individual people and single groups, might create initial bafflement or conflicts concerning social work purposes and the genuineness of professional commitment to the interest of those served. Flexibility made positive impressions. For example, an outstanding part of one student's field experience was the acceptance by a supervisor of the idiosyncrasies of the student's automobile in relation to arrival time at conference. Originally his lateness had been discussed in terms of student rejection of conference opportunity. What impressed the student was a ready apology when the reality of his efforts to meet his obligation was understood. A noticeable (to the student) change in his understanding of individuals and their handicaps followed during the next few weeks, and he was able to relax in his interpretation of (group work) agency demands. He saw social workers as "people who are continuously ready to see another's point of view."

2. *Beginnings of a Peer Culture*

Watching the action of recent graduates of schools in their first jobs was recalled by students as a satisfying and productive experience. They were also keenly conscious of the behavior of more advanced students. This seemed to be an attempt to establish a growth pattern and visualize a future occupational peer group not too remote but definitely professional in nature. They were particularly impressed by any group sharing of uncertainties concerning the management of a treatment situation or community problem; apparently this helped in the comprehension of social work as continual decision-making based on values.

A number of students thought early student activities were the greatest single influence in the learning of values, and important also in ethics. They were appreciative when the faculty left management of student groups entirely to students, even though they sensed that comment in student publications and some social action efforts might not have complete faculty acquiescence. "They really let us be self-determining," one said proudly.

3. *Membership in a Large Reference Group*

Social science indicates that values are learned not only through identification with parental and peer group images but also from the values held by reference groups with which the learner is associated.[2] The educational process immediately begins to introduce the student to a new reference group, his occupation, which for the rest of his lifetime will be one of the most powerful competing

[2] Roy Sorenson and Hedley S. Dimock, *Designing Education in Values* (New York: Association Press, 1955), 31, 39–41, 354; Robert K. Merton and Alice S. Kitt, "Contributions to the Theory of Reference Group Behavior," in *Continuities in Social Research,* ed. Robert K. Merton and Paul F. Lazarsfeld (Glencoe, Illinois: The Free Press, 1950), 40–105.

influences in his value-oriented decisions. Group experience to be influential in this way must be satisfying and frequent. Early opportunity for actual professional group interchange apart from field requirements is one of the most effectual means of communicating values. Evaluations, student interviews, and faculty experience showed that in the period of eagerness and enthusiasm, and to a lesser extent throughout the two school years, participation in local social work projects provided a *bona fide* taste of this kind of reference group interchange. A spontaneously organized student discussion group which met evenings without the presence of faculty, to discuss various hypotheses about the nature of man as they might be useful in social work, served in this way. Purchase of the beginning of a professional library and subscription to journals in his first semester was looked back upon by a fourth semester student as an experience of deep symbolic meaning which satisfied an early need to feel himself as a professional member.

Without any prodding, students very quickly begin to behave externally like the initial picture they receive of what a member of their new reference group is like. They also very early absorb impressions of the profession's negative values, "what is not done." In a Southern school, the earliest value learning one student could recall was the strange feeling of eating in a racially mixed dining hall. He was going to seek a separate table when he observed second-year students did not do so. Illustrations of the values expressed in the behavior of professional persons which students noted as seeming particularly impressive were:

> Responsibility in the keeping of promises on the part of faculty and field instructors. (All but one example were extremely positive.)
>
> Treatment of minority groups. (There were both negative and positive examples of this.)
>
> Acceptance of beliefs different from the social worker's own. (Again students also spoke of disillusion when they found ideas contrary to a teacher's personal values not well accepted.)

4. *The External Setting*

Reflecting the interests and ideals of the reference group, but somewhat different as a type of influence in establishing a sense of professional values, was the character of the physical plant itself, both in schools and agencies. There were many illustrations of response to pictures on walls, treatment of clients and students in waiting rooms. The author was told again and again of something in the environment, wordless and uncommented upon by teachers or supervisors, which had made a deep impression. A student visited another school than his own and came back questioning why the faculty of his own school did not belong to N.A.S.W. He had noticed framed membership certificates on the wall in the other school. Another noted the prominence given to wealthy contributors to endowment in contrast to distinguished faculty.

The actual learning content of all such experiences with "head men," "peers," "reference group," and physical characteristics of the setting ought to be weighed continuously. Breadth and catholicity of social work students, methods of participation with fellow practitioners in common enterprises, modes of communication appeared to be part of the content acquired in this manner. It may be possible to take greater advantage of the early orientation period with its intense desire *to be like* a social worker. In the beginning, behavior may be copying at an externally conforming level, but values acted out soon become comfortable, later automatic, and finally internalized as a kind of professional conscience.

Since this is bound to happen and occasionally can take place in a partial or destructive way rather than with optimum "by-product effect," it would seem that schools could insure that opportunities for group interchange and school decorations exemplify or even exaggerate the best examples of the external behavior they hope eventually to internalize.

Dangers in this type of "atmospheric" learning are that an external may be copied only in part or used out of context without related values to balance. In an effort to seem dignified, the student may become cold and artificial. He may copy brevity in telephone conversation by abrupt monosyllables. The best insurance against artificial copying probably is having a number of professional models to follow rather than a few. During this initial period a student makes certain he believes he will be comfortable in the profession he has chosen and that he can meet its external demands.

QUESTIONING AND DISILLUSIONMENT CONCERNING THE PROFESSION

After the initial exuberance at being a professional person, the second or uncertain, stage began, usually two to five months after arrival for both "good" and "poor" students. Students discovered that not all professional social workers behave according to the idealistic patterns they are being taught, and they saw behavior that to them seemed contrary to alleged values, or conspicuously unethical. They became discouraged at the small results apparent in terms of the immense needs they were finding at first hand. Many times this disillusionment stemmed from the fact that the social work behavior observed did not coincide with the student's narrow conception of a value. The use of authority might seem betrayal of the doctrine of self-determination. Sectarianism contradicted acceptance. Permitting a child to return to a home of limited advantages seemed a travesty on the social work conception of the good parent. Inadequate allowances did not meet "basic needs." The charging of fees denied service on a basis of equal availability to all. The main difficulty seemed to derive from the fact that, in both class and field, values and bits of ethical behavior were encountered as isolated phenomena without balance by other values equally approved by social work. One part of the curriculum appeared to them to contradict another; they did not perceive interrelationships. As one student put it in his school paper, "You are bound to be wrong." This was reflected in student skits and jokes and sayings in student peer culture. For example, "If you are on time, you're compulsive; if you are late, you're hostile; if you're early, it's over-anxiety."

In numerous ways concerted faculty planning can offset negative results of this disillusionment and serious questioning, and make positive use of it. To this author it seemed a healthy indication that genuine learning rather than copying was taking place. However, the many examples collected raise questions about the way in which early learning experiences may be balanced to give an integrated instead of fragmented initial picture of the totality of social work. Teaching values in constellations (see pages 44–45) offering potential stituations of varying character to compare with actual characteristics of the few in the field, making certain that students are aware of the many professional interests of their professional mentors, teaching as much of the curriculum as possible in groups mixed as to method and setting so that the profession is perceived as rounded in its concerns, all seemed to be ways in which students are assisted in their efforts to deal with these perplexities. Frank admission that as yet social work practice often exhibits many uncertainties and inconsistencies and that immediate results may not correspond to ideals, rather than any tendency to deny this or to defend limited accomplishments, was helpful. Successful students discovered ways of coming to terms with such problems, but all were enormously helped by a continuously positive picture of many social work facets and of the profession's efforts to achieve complete attainment of its goals.

QUESTIONING OF PERSONAL ABILITY TO REALIZE PROFESSIONAL VALUES

The third period occurs during the last three to five months. Students seemed to experience a feeling of panic that they did not know enough to practice independently, that their clients (individuals or groups) did not change at the rate they should. Instead of questioning the profession and its values as they were inclined to do earlier, they now more characteristically questioned their own ability to achieve professional ends. The rate of change in method worried a good many students; they wondered how long the skills they had mastered would prove useful.

This is a period when a study of ethics insofar as the profession has developed its formulations appeared to be reassuring and challenging. Students needed encouragement to feel there is an accumulation of group thinking which could be useful as a guide though not a directive when they had to make decisions more independently. The values of the profession could now be taught in summarized form as abstractions, as sub-concepts and as issues. For example, "respect for every individual" was seen in its relation to the confidential nature of professional relationship and also to race and class realities.

The concepts of partial fulfillment of ultimate goals, and the relative nature of "progress" and "change" seemed reassuring to students in their fourth semester. At this point, such concepts seem less a process of rationalization of professional shortcomings

and more in the nature of knowledgeable appraisal of social reality. "The profession" as an instrumental value could be stressed in
both backward and forward perspective—how far we have come,
and to what ideals the profession seems to be moving. Most students at this time were working on theses and characteristically
were struggling with the importance of scientific discovery and
validation in the social work field. Finding out that "the profession" as yet has to work with many uncertainties, seemed to reassure individual students that they would be able to deal with their
own. Grasping as a value the possibility of continuous perfecting
of understanding and skill, with each professional member making
his contribution, seemed to act as an antidote to the stage fright
accompanying search and planning for his first job.

Symbolic evidence of confidence in them as *professional* people
had particular meaning to students at this point. One student
graphically described the way he had progressively gained confidence in his own understanding of social work, and his increased
feeling that he could later use his understanding, as he participated
in a seminar where situations in a variety of settings were reviewed
from the standpoint of the professional values involved ("what the
profession was aiming at") and the ethical obligations which must
be observed ("how a social worker ethically can help get there").
He stressed the value to him of seeing that "the same things hold
true" in many situations; it gave him the feeling that, as he met
new types of problems, his field experience would still be applicable. The "tone" of the seminar had most meaning to him. It was a
demonstration that the faculty believed the class was ready to
consider fundamental professional issues. "It was almost like a
staff meeting."

Commitment to specific professional values, including the value
that the profession is effectively helping to achieve their ultimate
realization, appeared to be the best means of helping students
through the period of final panic to a conception of themselves as
well-equipped professional people. The idea that the questioning
of values and the degree to which they were being achieved was
legitimate and approved by the profession, especially if done in an
orderly research manner, also helped the student overcome his
panic and feeling of need for certainty.

LEVELS OF UNDERSTANDING OF VALUES

Consideration of each student's value formation is a useful component in any educational diagnosis. Oftentimes summarized in evaluations or faculty comment as "suitable attitudes" or "good identification with the profession," a breakdown into specific aspects would seem to have much more meaning for planning in the educational process. In the education of adults, educational experiences must be geared to various levels of value incorporation. Perhaps Jack L. Rubins' suggestions [3] for levels of religious attitudes (belief, faith, ritual) might be suggestive in considering other values as well. For any single student, some values are a matter of intellectual affirmation or conviction as to their rightness, backed by empirically collected data; others take on an emotional quality of devoted adherence without much reasoning process; still others are a matter of outward form and conformance; the most compelling values include all three elements. With "democracy," for instance, conviction as to the essential "rightness" of equal participation may be based on the fact that it works better than other forms and that men have been shown to be potentially equal in their ability to participate in their own society. Or an emotional feeling about the importance of democracy may have been engendered by various emphases on patriotism in group ceremonies in childhood or by personal experience with frustration at having been denied full participation. Democracy may be associated with ritualistic forms such as voting, fair representation, rigid observance of majority rule.

This suggests the possibility that personal conflict in learning may occur when new intellectual experiences provide different interpretations which conflict with emotional or ritualistic perceptions of values, or when more varied ritualistic forms are offered as examples of emotionally or intellectually comprehended forms.

[3] Jack L. Rubins, "Neurotic Attitudes Toward Religion," *American Journal of Psychoanalysis,* XV, 1 (1955), 71–81. See also Sorenson, and Dimock, *op. cit.,* 39, which lists the elements in the operation of values as the intellectual, emotional, volitional and behavior factors, and Florence Rockwood Kluckhohn, "Dominant and Variant Value Orientations," in *Personality in Nature, Society, and Culture,* eds. Kluckhohn and Murray, *op. cit.,* 342–357 for discussion of patterning of variations in orientation to values.

A teacher often sees a value from one point of view while a student's basic orientation is mainly of another kind. A student was inclined to put pressure on a group to accept what seemed to be majority opinion, when the group tended to be permissive, and grant a minority considerable influence in choosing a program. This student's level of functioning with respect to that value was highly ritualistic and somewhat intellectual. He had to be helped by the field teacher to see that the feeling tone of the group, in its relaxed willingness to share and take turns, was also "democratic."

The student has to learn that what, for him, may be a value of high emotional commitment as well as intellectual affirmation, may for someone else be a matter of outward form which can be modified by substituting other satisfying ritualistic practices with relatively little emotional strain. In learning how to handle his own personality in a professional way, part of his development of self-awareness is self-discovery of the quality and level of many of his own values. Since the consensus of social work educational thinking seems to lean to the opinion that the educator does not act in the role of therapist,[4] who deals with deeply internalized personality patterns, growth of much of this self-understanding may be stimulated by intellectual comprehension of how values are formed and various levels into which they may develop. Appraising value formation of clients in order to understand them will involve practice in student handling of his own values. In supervisory reports of one student's progress, a large step forward came when he discovered attendance at religious services was not viewed as equally obligatory by all groups. Emotional devotion and intellectual acceptance were given high priorities by some. Urging a delinquent to go to church then was seen as lacking in respect for that client's value system.

VARIATIONS IN LEARNING PATTERNS[5]

Equally intelligent, sensitive, warm learners approached values in two ways. Some found it easiest to think of an idealistic abstraction

[4] Towle, *op. cit.*, 145.
[5] Sol Wiener Ginsburg, "The Impact of the Social Worker's Cultural Structure on Social Therapy," *op. cit.*, and Sol Wiener Ginsburg, "Values and the Psychiatrist," *American Journal of Orthopsychiatry*, XX, 3 (July, 1950), 466–478.

to which they had long been taught to have emotionalized devotion, and were then pleased to discover many new concrete exemplifications in the context of their new occupational orbit. Others proceeded from what they felt some individual or group situation demanded and were intellectually enthused to find that in the process of providing the service indicated, they were augmenting some abstract value. "Good housing is respect for human dignity," one delighted student exclaimed when he helped a family move. "I was partializing and didn't know it," marvelled another, whose supervisor took advantage of his exhilaration at learning to identify the abstractions he was hearing about by some discussion of his role as a worker in helping his client sort out personal goals into manageable units of purposive activity.

A danger seemed to arise when in either approach the other was not also *included at the same time*. Some methods teachers are frustrated if a broadly philosophic question is posed such as "What will the use of this technique do to other people in the situation if it makes the client a different person? Will it result in divorce?" Some philosophy-ethics teachers in professional seminars hesitate to take time to consider individual or group problems which students present, in their feeling of urgency to get to large basic problems. Since both types of students appear in both types of classes, learning experiences involving both modes of presentation ought to be included in every type of course. Field teachers probably have greatest opportunity to sense which mode of approach makes the most vivid impression on an individual student and utilize it to accustom the student to both.

From the standpoint of the learner, either approach may appear as fragmented. Poor students showed both tendencies, often using one or the other approach to escape from integrated learning. Failure to meet a specific situation adequately might be rationalized on the basis that long-range social reform was required because of the way society had failed their clients. Frequently learning from one situation was not transferred to others or incorporated in class papers because broad implications and large goals were not identified as such. In an effort to interest a pre-delinquent natural group in agency facilities, inducement in the form of concession to agency rules was offered by a student field worker. The effect of rule-abiding groups already incorporated and deriving benefit was not taken into account. Reference by a supervisor to the principle that both general social good and individual need had to be considered helped that student sense his ethical obligations to agency and community.

Sol Ginsburg's descriptions of the professional ideal for the psychiatrist would also hold true as an educational aim for the social worker—achievement of "recognized subjectivity." A student should learn in what way he tends to regard a situation where values may be concerned—as an opportunity to implement a high-level value, or as a problem to be worked out in terms of the immediacy of apparent needs, keeping proximate values in mind.

In developing objectives for the total learning process, and in considering the usefulness of each learning experience, the author believes stages in learning, levels of value incorporation, and characteristic learning patterns all must be considered. Students in a typical stage may be at various levels of value development with respect to different values. To achieve professional handling of choices between values, many combinations of stages, levels, and learning patterns must be provided for in the content presented.

CHAPTER V

Educational Objectives for the Teaching of Values and Ethics

In tabulating the many descriptions of "good" social work behavior from all the materials assembled in this project,[1] ten distinct types of behavior dependent upon an orientation to values and ethics finally emerged as they were grouped and regrouped.[2] The content of the curriculum and total school experience must provide for developing such patterns of thinking and acting in students so that professional social workers can be counted upon ordinarily to behave in these ways. They thus become the major objectives of the educational process with respect to values and ethics.

For each objective there is a body of information, verified theoretical knowledge and speculation which illumines understanding of the place of values and ethically selected behavior in all professional relationships, and on which a practitioner relies for guidance and suggestion in making his own choices as he conducts the helping process.

In addition to this specific knowledge content, it appeared that each of the behaviors in the ten objectives comes into play in three areas of professional life.[3]

First, that part which is carried on in *relating the values of the profession to those operating in the culture at large*—the social worker's comprehension of differences and similarities and his response to them as they affect his services to persons, groups and communities. Second, that part of professional life which has to do with *internal*

[1] See Chapter II (34–35).
[2] See Introduction (5).
[3] Originally four areas were used also to include relationship to "agency," but it was found in classification process that every example of "agency" relationships was either a matter of ultimately relating to the culture in the community via board, to colleagues (his superior, supervisee, administrator, etc.), or to clientele. Material regarding agency has therefore been so incorporated. "Agency" appeared to be an instrument through which relationships in these fundamental areas could be effected.

relationships within the professional membership—sharpening and clarifying values as the profession interprets and implements them, following modes of sharing them with colleagues through professional lines of communication, participating as a member of professional organizations in preserving and enhancing them.

Third, that part of professional performance which has to do with *relations to the specific groups or individuals served*—understanding the values of the clientele and the problems they confront in regard to preserving the values, comprehension of the place of values in the process by which helping and problem-solving is accomplished in a professionally ethical way.

Content objectives thus should include material needed to acquaint the prospective social worker with the nature of professional interchange with the general culture, colleagues, and clientele. Each behavior was examined to see what a social worker needs to know about the way professional values and ethics operate in these three areas.

Each objective, therefore, is presented as a comprehensive statement discussed under two major headings—the available related knowledge content and the three areas of professional life where it would be applied, with illustrations drawn from project data. The number of pertinent illustrations coming to light in project materials, and the volume of related facts and theory varied. Often the same basic knowledge was found to be usable in several types of situations and helpful in obtaining several objectives. Future faculty experimentation, a detailed study of practice, and a much more detailed examination of philosophic and social science materials would no doubt reveal more pertinent and extensive content than the scope of this project could cover in the limited time available. Related curriculum content is therefore suggestive rather than exhaustive in coverage.

OBJECTIVE I:

Comprehension of Values, Disvalues and Ethical Judgments as Human Phenomena Understanding the Philosophic-Spiritual Component in Every Life Situation [4]

RELATED KNOWLEDGE

A part of the understanding of people, which is an essential in all of social work, is to be aware that every human being operates in relation to some sort of philosophy of life.[5] The fact that individuals and groups cherish their own value positions is part of the reality within which the social worker must perform. Dynamic psychology, anthropology, sociology, and philosophy all have produced theoretic material which shows how values influence external and internal behavior. Examples of such illuminating background knowledge are:

1. *Theory with Respect to Value Formation*

There are two major ideas about the ways in which values have

[4] For definition of values, disvalues, and ethical judgment as here used see Chapter II, 23. In this sense, "comprehension" is used as an all-inclusive apprehension or identification of diverse manifestations under one general impression. "Understanding" implies acceptance as a settled fact in existence and observed human living.

[5] Material on the nature of the value component is a synthesized summary drawn chiefly from: Felix P. Biestek, S.J., "Religion and Social Casework," in *The Social Welfare Forum, 1956* (New York: National Conference of Social Work by Columbia University Press, 1956), 86–95; David Bidney, "The Concept of Value in Modern Anthropology," in *Anthropology Today,* ed. A. L. Kroeber *et al.* (Chicago: University of Chicago Press, 1953); Werner W. Boehm, "Social Work and the Social Sciences," *Journal of Psychiatric Social Work,* XXI, 1 (September, 1951), 4–8; K. E. Boulding, "Some Contributions of Economics to the General Theory of Value," *Philosophy of Science,* XXIII, 1 (January, 1956), 1–14; George W. Hartman, "Value as the Unifying Concept of the Social Sciences," *Journal of Social Psychology,* X, 4 (November, 1939), 563–575; Morris, *op. cit.;* Gunner Myrdal, *An American Dilemma* (New York: Harper & Bros., 1944). Appendix 1, "Note on Valuation and Beliefs," 1027–1034. Appendix 2, "A Methodological Note on Facts and Valuations in Social Science," 1035–1070; Ralph Barton Perry, *Realms of Value* (Cambridge, Mass.: Harvard University Press, 1954); Pratt, "The Nature of Value," in *Science, Philosophy and Religion,* ed. Lyman Bryson and Louis Finkelstein (New York: Conference on Science, Philosophy and Religion, 1943); Oliver L. Reiser, "Postulates for an Ethics of Belief in Science, Religion, and Philosophy," *Philosophy of Science,* XXIII, 14 (October, 1956), 280–282; M. Roshwald, "Value-Judgments in the Social Sciences," *The British Journal for the Philosophy of Science,* VI (November, 1955), 186–208; Sue Spencer, "Religion and Social Work," *Social Work,* I, 3 (July, 1956), 19–26; Robin M. Williams, Jr., *American Society* (New York: Alfred A. Knopf, 1951).

developed over the ages.[6] Much of mankind believes that ultimate values have been ordained by supernatural forces beyond man's powers of observation or full understanding and are fixed and unchanging laws of the universe, comparable to laws concerning the physical environment. Man must learn to come to terms with them by changing himself to conform and by discovering new information about their meaning and intent. Others believe that values have grown only from human experience with what works and doesn't work in the ever-changing processes of living; values can, therefore, be eliminated or altered as circumstances demand. In the course of human existence, these two ideas have interacted, reinforcing and at times conflicting with each other, so that now there are unnumbered gradations and combinations of these two central ideas.

Groups which adhere to a fixed value system with respect to ultimate values often follow the process of pragmatic discovery of "what works" with respect to subsidiary or instrumental values, so long as standards so attained do not deny those of the fixed system. They often produce concrete objective experience or scientific corroboration which they believe illustrates the validity and working effectiveness of ordained values.

Conversely, persons who believe that human experience alone determines values sometimes view man and his abilities in a highly mystical way. Others believe supernatural forces govern some life processes as yet incomprehensible to man's understanding, while experience should govern others which are subject to objective scrutiny. Some think all values will be determined in the future wholly by scientifically validated experiment; science then takes on a near magical meaning of supreme importance.

Anyone working with people must sense that each human being has to have some mechanisms for dealing with unknown mysteries of the universe; for finding purpose and meaning in life; for explaining satisfactions, disappointments, and seeming inequities. In order to work with a particular person or group it is necessary to

6 See Biestek, "Religion and Social Casework," op. cit.; Florence Rockwood Kluckhohn, "Dominant and Variant Value Orientations," in Personality in Nature, Society, and Culture, ed. by Kluckhohn and Murray, op. cit.; Morris, op. cit.; Reiser, op. cit.; Williams, "Religion, Value Orientations, and Intergroup Conflict," op. cit., for an idea of the range of philosophic beliefs growing out of these two approaches.

understand the basis of that person's or group's sense of what is desirable and undesirable.

In the opinion of this author, it is also necessary to comprehend that in spite of many variations and some overlapping, in which groups believing in supernatural origins utilize human experience in many instances and humanistically or scientifically oriented groups develop mystical tendencies, the two views of value formation, carried to their ultimate conclusions, are essentially irreconcilable.[7] When forced to a final choice of vital nature, decisions of approval, or disapproval are usually made in terms of one or the other. Each group answers the proposals of the other in terms of its own value system. Neither is convinced its position is refuted.[8] Both believe that the other group is depriving itself of opportunities for fuller living by the limitations of its positions, and deceiving itself with its major assumptions.

In examining student field work, there were many illustrations where failure to understand the origin of underlying assumptions on which a client or community group was operating caused a student to perceive the client as limited, unintelligent, or stubborn. A humanist regarded a devout Christian's view of the dissolubility of marriage as impractical and ungrounded, in view of many "successful" divorces. A Catholic was unable to work with a couple whose marriage took place before a justice. Both these students used social work's belief in the primacy of good family life as justification for their positions, and found it difficult to analyze the situations in terms of the client's values rather than their own.

[7] Williams, "Religion, Value Orientations, and Intergroup Conflict," *op. cit.*

[8] For the question of the relation of scientific validation and revelation of the supernatural, see Kenneth D. Benne, and G. E. Swanson, "The Problem of Values and the Social Scientist," *Journal of Social Issues,* VI, 4 (1950), 2–7; Raymond B. Battell, "Ethics and the Social Sciences," *The American Psychologist,* III (June, 1948), 193–198; Raymond B. Cattell, "The Integration of Psychology with Moral Values," *The British Journal of Psychology,* XLI (September, 1950), 25–33; C. West Churchman, "Sciences and Decision Making, *Philosophy of Science,* XXIII, 3 (July, 1956), 247–249; Abraham Edel, *Ethical Judgment: The Use of Science in Ethics* (New York: Free Press, 1955); Herbert Feigl, "An Analysis of the Nature and the Limits of Ethical Arguments," mimeographed: Hartman, *op. cit.;* Charles R. McKenney, *Moral Problems in Social Work* (Milwaukee: Bruce Publishing Co., 1951); Robert Palter, "Philosophic Principles and Scientific Theory," *Philosophy of Science,* XXIII, 2 (April, 1956), 111–135; Talcott Parsons, Edward A. Shils, and James Olds, "Values, Motives, and Systems of Action," in *Toward a General Theory of Action,* ed. T. Parsons and E. A. Shils (Cambridge, Mass.: Harvard University Press, 1951); Pratt, *op. cit.;* Reiser, *op. cit.;* Roshwald, *op. cit.*

Both had to consider the question of origin in the problem of validation of values.

In practical matters, adherents of both positions show wide agreement on much human conduct which is considered acceptable or most desirable, as well as on that which is unacceptable. Cardinal virtues such as honesty, loyalty, compassion are venerated by both groups because they have been given supernatural sanction and seem to work in human relations. The social worker must be able to recognize in any situation whether it can be dealt with on this practical level of substantial agreement (regardless of origin), whether it is in an area where both groups believe the results of human experimentation can be the governing factor in immediate decisions, or whether it relates to one of the substantially different explanations of the origin of values. Failure to identify the nature of such differences may cause clouding of issues and obscuring or slowing of partial solutions, with a perpetuation of conflicts and resentments beneath the surface of individual or community life.

2. *General Types of Value Manifestation*

As part of his perception of the reality with which he is dealing, a social worker should be able to recognize various ways in which individuals and the society at large express values, such as:

a. Goals and Aspirations. Many values are identified by expressed hopes of what might be attained. Such statements on the part of those he works with give the social worker an idea of what the client considers of most worth.

b. Rituals, Customary Forms, Manners. Repeated behavior often indicates to what value orientation a client has been exposed. Outward ritual is (or was originally) symbolic of something desirable and to be attained or undesirable and to be avoided.

c. Rights. This implies that the individual or group has a claim to appropriate certain material goods or to act in a certain manner which may be enforced against other individuals, groups, or society itself. In a sense rights are guarantees that values can be made accessible to persons who cherish them.

d. Duties, Obligations, Accountability. Constraining feelings on the part of groups that they are bound to act in certain ways, and that their actions must be explained to others, are usually expressed in such words as "should," "ought," "must," "have to," and describe both limitations and requirements. What may be optional in one value system may be highly obligatory in another; what one system may consider highly personal, another may believe is subject to accountability to authority. To understand his clients the social worker must identify what the individuals and groups he deals with feel "duty bound" to do.

e. Sanctions. Approval of an act indicated by reward or recognition, or disapproval indicated by blame, punishment or humiliation; social acceptance or sponsorship of an activity, or refusal to grant sponsorship. The desire to punish often indicates an underlying value. In helping communities and individuals, the social worker often has to help them discover helpful means of exerting sanctions of the same value previously expressed in sanctions that caused harm (according to social work values).

f. Value Conflicts. Competition among several desirable values for priority in determining a course of action. Such competition may occur between different individuals or groups holding opposing values, or between differing values held by a single individual or group. Often the clearest way to discover what a group's most impelling values may be is to observe what they ridicule, oppose, or fight for.

3. *Principles Concerning the Operation of Values*

Value theorists have developed much speculation and some experimentally validated material on how values become part of the ongoing social process.[9] Some such principles of which a social worker should be aware, are: [10]

[9] Clyde Kluckhohn, "Values and Value Orientation in the Theory of Action," in *Toward a General Theory of Action,* ed. Talcott Parsons and Edward A. Shils (Cambridge, Mass.: Harvard University Press, 1951), 388–433; Kluckhohn and Murray, "Personality Formation: The Determinants," in *Personality in Nature, Society, and Culture, op. cit.;* Florence Rockwood Kluckhohn, "Dominant and Variant Value Orientations," in *Personality in Nature, Society, and Culture,* ed. Kluckhohn and Murray, *op. cit.;* Parsons, Shils, and Old, "Values, Motives, and Systems of Action," in *Toward a General Theory of Action,* ed. Parsons and Shils, *op. cit.;* Sorenson and Dimock, *op. cit.,* 24–50.
[10] The author is indebted to the Panel on Values and Ethics for most of these suggestions and the form in which they are developed.

a. Values are learned in interpersonal cultural interaction approved parentally, by reference groups, or the general cultural milieu.

b. Groups may hold the same values but assign different priorities to them.

c. Values are usually found in constellations of similarities and opposites.

d. Values are integrated at different levels—verbal, action, feeling, and commitment.

e. Values are expressed in abstractions of varying levels, including the means to attain highly abstract values.

4. *The Dynamic Functions of Values*

There are many opinions as to just how values function in human life. Some take the position that they have a strengthening and stimulating effect; others see negative characteristics in the inhibiting of change or stifling of variability. Social work literature, field work reports, and class audits pointed to the following as typical social work understandings:

a. In Ego Formation of the Individual. Values are the basis on which the person selects and approves or disapproves his own behavior and that of others, a major component in the psychoanalytic conception of Superego and of Conscience in religious terminology. Hence guilt, self-satisfaction and intra-personal conflicts are all dependent on values to which the individual has been exposed, to which he has chosen to adhere, or among which he is trying to make choice.[11]

b. In Group Solidarity. The holding, cherishing and defending of values is one of the forces which bind people together in groups, communities, and political states. In small groups, the development of informal codes; in primitive communities, early law and mores; in complex communities, formalized law and "public

11 Cattell, "Ethics and the Social Sciences," *op. cit.;* Cattell, "The Integration of Psychology with Moral Values," *op. cit.;* Dan W. Dodson, "Moral and Ethical Values" [Notes on speech given in Workshop on Moral and Ethical Values, Committee on Youth Services, National Social Welfare Assembly, June 6, 1957.]; Ginsburg, "Values and the Psychiatrist," *op. cit.;* A. Irving Hallowell, "Values, Acculturation and Mental Health," *American Journal of Orthopsychiatry,* XX, 4 (October, 1950), 732–743.

opinion" all represent selected values which unite and activate people.[12]

c. In the Formation of Professions. Agreed upon ends, means, and approved personal behavior are a binding force in a professional body. (See Chapter I.) The social worker needs to know the value system and value priorities of his own profession and also to be familiar with those of the professions and occupational groups with which he must deal.

APPLICATION IN PROFESSIONAL LIFE

The theoretic material from the social sciences and philosophic disciplines concerning value formation, value manifestation, value principles, and dynamic functions of values helps the social worker comprehend the operation of values in every life situation, as he operates in the three areas of professional performance. The curriculum must also help the student identify professional situations where the theory may be illuminating.

Relation to the Cultural Milieu—Such comprehension enables the social worker to place social work as a part of the total culture. He must be able to distinguish when preferred social work behavior is supported by values common in the society, when general cultural values are unrelated or may prove either positive or negative depending on circumstances, and when values in the culture are hostile to the values cherished by social work.[13] A community organization worker realized that a budget committee was conflicted over whether to give money to an agency which was welcoming a new immigrant group that members resented having in the community. He was able to help them sort out the relative weight of the values involved, such as the right of all persons to opportunity, the meaning of democracy, self-maximation, personal and racial superiority, and intimate in-group neighborliness and pride.

The worker must perceive how social work customs and ap-

12 Bidney, *op. cit.*; Kluckhohn, "Values and Value Orientation in the Theory of Action," in *Toward a General Theory of Action*, ed. Parsons and Shils, *op. cit.*; Florence Rockwood Kluckhohn, "Dominant and Variant Value Orientations," in *Personality in Nature, Society, and Culture*, ed. Kluckhohn and Murray, *op. cit.*
13 This is a paraphrase of the conclusion of one subcommittee of the panel and was regarded as highly significant by the whole panel.

proaches relate to common community conceptions of ethical behavior such as "fair play," "abiding by the rules of the game," "prevention of distress." [14]

He must be able to recognize when general cultural values as expressed at verbal level take on special priorities in significance, amplified meaning or unique manifestations in social work. For example, "human rights" in social work may mean the right to satisfaction of basic needs through taxation if necessary; to others in the culture it may mean the right to limit taxation and retain all the personal economic gains possible for personal use. The social worker must also be able to recognize when his social work goals coincide or conflict with those of his colleagues, both lay persons and members of other professions.

Relation to Members of the Profession—Value theory helps social work practitioners to perceive social work as a sub-culture,[15] and to understand some of its internally conflicting values. These often arise out of its historic derivation from social movements having roots both in the supernatural and pragmatic traditions,[16] with both major strands placing high value on scientific validation of the institutional means social work devises to attain its ends. An awareness of the range and varying quality of values would help the professional person become aware of the multiple personal value commitments which all members of the profession are constantly trying to reconcile with commonly held social work aspirations. For example, an N.A.S.W. student member was puzzled over conflict regarding the organization's support of new child welfare laws until cultural differences in the backgrounds and basic value systems among members were pointed out. Then it became clear that some members did not place first priority on the religious nurture of the child and some did. Others made protection of the community from anti-social children a first priority while some saw development of the delinquent himself as a primary goal.

[14] Suggestion of the *Ad Hoc* Panel.
[15] Greenwood, *op. cit.*
[16] Karl deSchweinitz, "Social Values and Social Action—the Intellectual Base as Illustrated in the Study of History," *Social Service Review*, XXX, 2 (June, 1956), 119–131.

Relation to Clientele—Theoretical knowledge regarding values helps deepen the insight which enables a social worker during the exploratory phases of the helping process to appraise the functioning of the client, whether individual, group or community. He should be able to identify rigidity, certainty, anomie, conflicting or poorly formulated value formations, and to sense when a client is seeking help in understanding the values of others or in clarifying his own positions. For example, a mental patient long estranged from his national and religious groups was hospitalized in a state of disintegration characterized by an absence of any values. A student social worker in the hospital, alert to this aspect of his condition, sensed that in reality he was longing to see a religious advisor and facilitated his doing so.

In our complex society, in any sub-culture, even a socially isolated one, most people are exposed to several reference groups.[17] For any individual certain values may take on an "absolute," "unbending" character while others may be more in the nature of unthinking imitation of "what others are doing." A union member might choose a union meeting instead of a church service or follow behavior norms which his religious advisor would consider of dubious ethical stature. Some people will sacrifice "health" for "education;" some will relinquish immediate material comfort for future social advancement. Seeing that such behaviors are characteristic human phenomena enables the social worker to take into account this aspect of his client's interests and external behavior as well as to understand more fully the nature of pressures and conflicts which the client is facing.

In the later stages of working with his clients the worker has to know how to help the client implement his own values, tap value sources he is seeking,[18] assert his right and meet his obligations.

---

[17] Merton and Kitt, "Contributions to the Theory of Reference Group Behavior," in *Continuities in Social Research*, ed. Merton and Lazarsfeld, *op. cit.*
[18] For the use of values as resources see Nathan W. Ackerman, "Mental Hygiene and Social Work, Today and Tomorrow," *Social Casework*, XXXVI, 2 (February, 1955), 63–73; Biestek, "Religion and Social Casework," *op. cit.*; Joseph W. Eaton, "How Values Affect Social Practice." (Typewritten); Elizabeth Gaynor, "Religion as a Resource in the Adjustment of Catholic Patients Following Hospitalization for a Mental Illness." (Unpublished Master's project; New York School of Social Work, Columbia University, 1949); Ginsburg, "The Impact of the Social Worker's Cultural Structure on Social Therapy," *op. cit.*; Goldsmith, *op. cit.*

The worker must be able to determine when groups differ as to means but have a common end in view; when they agree on a useful means but differ about the end to which it should be directed or what group should assume responsibility for its implementation.

Student field experiences and records used in teaching showed that much helping involves stimulating clients to make a new appraisal of priorities—postponing immediate satisfaction of one value in favor of later attainment of another, deepening commitment to values from a verbal to action level, finding numerous possible means of attainment instead of one fixed but perhaps inaccessible way.

Frequently in working with communities the helping process is a matter of determining priorities or coming to some type of compromise among different ideas as to priorities. All social work involves establishing immediate goals which are realistically possible in the near future, but related to more distant ones.

All of this material on value theory and its application in the three areas of professional life would constitute the knowledge base for attaining the other nine educational objectives also. Comprehension of the nature and function of values and ethical norms in human experience is essential before additional materials and experiences can be offered to help the social worker learn to behave in the following other ways found to be useful. What is said under the following objectives assumes that this basic theoretical structure is being made familiar to the student, and will not be repeated under each.

OBJECTIVE II:

Appreciation [19] of Different Value Systems Including His Own

RELATED KNOWLEDGE

1. *Group Goals*

A knowledge of and sensitivity to the goals which major religious, political and social groups are trying to attain—what each

[19] "Appreciation" is here used as sensitivity to distinctions, particularly the distinguishing positive aspects of any life experience—the sense of esteem and respect in forming any judgment.

group *sees itself* trying to do to enhance fulfillment—is required.[20]

It is important that this appreciation be related to the adherent's own conception and the variations within larger groupings, rather than to stereotyped conceptions of outer impressions or to carica- tures that exaggerate a single or atypical aspect.

2. *Accessibility of Values*

One mode of appreciation is awareness of how each value becomes available to its adherents, *e.g.,* democracy may be real for some groups only in relation to participation in policy formation, politi- cal choices, and contributions to political thought. Some religions lay emphasis on private meditation, some on reading from au- thorities, and others on contact with a mediator who can expedite an individual's relationship with supernatural power. To suggest to a member of a Friends Meeting that perhaps he would like to see his religious advisor would show lack of appreciation of how his values become real to him, while to a Roman Catholic it might symbolize sensitivity to his inner needs. Some groups may share values with others only through prescribed ritualistic means (*e.g.,* lodges) while others welcome new adherents on any show of inter- est.

3. *Characteristics of Values Which Make Them Useful in the Helping Process*

It is very difficult for a person who does not affirm a value for him- self to appreciate the positive potential it may represent for some- one else. Social treatment is enhanced if such possibilities are understood. The nature of each value also involves disadvantages and risks which must be taken into account. It appeared to be far easier for students to see the disadvantages in value systems (even their own) than the advantages, judging from field reports. Strange or bizarre externals made a deeper impression than the supportive and motivating aspects. Since much helping depends on utilizing positives, the affirmative aspects of each value system ought to be genuinely appreciated in terms of their meaning to those holding them.

[20] Williams, "Religion, Value Orientations, and Intergroup Conflict," *op. cit.;* Sister Frances Jerome Woods, *Cultural Values of American Ethnic Groups* (New York: Harper & Brothers, 1956).

Many aspects of value systems may have both positive and negative implications for the helping process, depending on how they are being used. The advantages in reliance on a supernatural system may be a feeling of certainty and direction, and an inner security at having an outside power on which to rely. Adherents may have a feeling of release of personal creativity in certain areas because part of their life decisions are handled by outside authority. This kind of security may be utilized as a positive force in helping. All theoretical material concerning usefulness of freedom within limits may be applicable. Negatively, fixed system may create a feeling of entrapment, exaggerated guilt, over-conformity, feelings of lack of opportunity for personal creativity or experiment, a need to struggle and resist in order to establish personal or group identity.

Pluralistic systems give their adherents a sense of adventure, of being able to absorb any new experience and idea, a zest for experimentation and innovation. Such systems, which advocate change as human discovery and inclination may indicate, can also result in a sense of normlessness, of no ties or guidelines on which an individual can rely. If experimentation proves disadvantageous, disillusionment, self-defeat, and cessation of effort can result.

It is important that social workers appreciate that both fixed and pluralistic beliefs may assume rigid aspects, or may permit wide variation within prescribed limits. Pluralistic systems may result in intolerance of intolerance, rigidity in non-conformity. An appreciation of the areas of latitude and the areas of absolute patterning of value norms helps in the understanding of groups and individuals.

With respect to any individual or group, often certain values are rigidly fixed while others permit wide variation. Similar advantages and disadvantages may arise from authoritarian and adaptive social and political systems. As part of his management of the helping relationship a worker must be able to help clients (individual, group, community) determine how much authority and rigidity and how much variation they wish to seek for a comfortable and constructive organization of individual, family and group life.

APPLICATION IN PROFESSIONAL LIFE

Relation to the Cultural Milieu—This kind of appreciation of the goals, means, methods of accessibility, hazards and advantages for personality and group growth, of value systems helps the social worker assess how different groups are using or are giving priorities to different goals or different means for attaining common ends. It gives indication of whether there is possibility of developing cooperation on the basis of commonality of ultimate purpose, of seeking a compromise through immediate proximate goals, of utilizing strengths in many systems positively instead of at cross purposes and conflict. (For instance, stability and variability may be values several systems can provide in varying degree and so help achieve balance in social interaction.) It helps the worker see the need for preserving old values as well as encouraging experimentation with new ones.

One community organizer was able to secure the interest, financial support, and personal effort of widely varying segments of the community with respect to studying the needs of aging people. He utilized the ideas both of those who wanted planning vested in voluntary and religious groups and of those who wanted immediate governmental participation. All were able first to get together on a plan for unattached, ill women, since their need appealed to many types of motivation—religious obligation, community self-respect, conformance to tradition, and so on.

Relation to Members of the Profession—The value systems of subgroups within the profession give indication of how difference can be handled without damage to the clientele. A worker should know the areas where concerted professional action is feasible and the areas where individual or sub-group action is indicated or can be defined, *e.g.,* groups with known high priority values with regard to pacifism would not be expected to contribute to professional thinking on the training of social workers for service for the armed forces, but might contribute their experience with non-resistance to the resolution of intergroup tensions. The political philosophies or party affiliations of members may be used both positively and negatively.

Mutual respect for other members of the profession is generated by a positive appreciation of what reference groups to which they belong are trying to do, even though there may be question of the means they select.

Relation to Clientele—In order to identify and understand what an individual or group sees as its problem it is necessary to understand what its aspirations are and the priorities among them. In any effort to stimulate change an appreciation of the operating value systems helps the worker understand what the change would cost the client in emotional or community strain.

A component which has a high priority in our professional image of the "good" social worker is "acceptance" of all kinds of people.[21] One aspect of it is appreciation of what another's value system may mean to him, or of the damaging effect conflicts of values or absence of orderly orientation to values may exert. In gauging treatment goals, some realization of values which it will be a sacrifice for a person or group to relinquish, such as "rugged individualism," "self-sufficiency at all costs," "prominence in the power structure," may help the worker show understanding of stresses clients are undergoing. A student was much impressed when a supervisor helped him see what moving out of a neighborhood being torn down for model housing meant to the people there. The values of improved external living conditions were not compensatory for values of group feeling and community identity.

Our profession has come to lay great stress on the professional self as an instrumental means in helping, so much so that the helping self has assumed many of the aspects of an instrumental value. It is spoken of with reverence and awe, referred to with assumed mutual understanding of its importance, and given high priority in educational and agency goals. Essentially, judging from implied

21 Felix P. Biestek, S.J., "The Non-Judgmental Attitude," *Social Casework*, XXXIV, 6 (June, 1953), 235–239; Felix P. Biestek, S.J., *The Principle of Client Self-Determination in Social Casework* (Washington, D.C.: The Catholic University of America Press, 1951); John J. Honigmann, "Toward a Distinction Between Psychiatric and Social Abnormality," *Social Forces*, XXXI, 3 (March, 1953), 274–277; Margery Kohl Hunt, "Integrating the Non-Judgmental Attitude with Social Responsibility and Authority in Social Casework" (Unpublished Master's thesis, School of Social Work, Universnty of Connecticut, 1957); Miriam McCaffery, "Criteria for Student Progress in Field Work," *Journal of Social Casework*, XXVII, (January, 1947), 9–17.

and defined meanings heard in audits, the notion of the professional self as a value stems from the pervading conviction that persons can be helped by active, purposeful behavior of a skilled professional person. The various components of the instrumental value "professional self," as related to values and ethics, were frequently referred to in student evaluations. A related value of "self-knowledge" was often mentioned. Knowledge of the formation of values, of various kinds and levels of values in others, helps the worker become aware of his own definitions of the desirable and undesirable.[22]

Much of our professional ethical thinking is based on the fact that, with our knowledge of the client and of ourselves, skillful handling of a relationship can influence the behavior of others, but that this *skill cannot be abused*. We do not deny nor do we forcefully impose our values. We do not force people back to former value positions or insist on the worker's, but help them discover values of meaning for them. An appreciation of many value systems aids a worker to use his own value system positively as part of himself, in the service of the client.

Psychiatric and clinical psychology writings as well as social work authorities point out that phenomena of relationship and transference might make it wholly possible for a worker to influence a person or group to do something "wrong" in the eyes of society, or according to the group's own value system. Professional ethics demands a controlled use of this power to influence behavior. This ethical principle is part of the content of social work which an aspiring professional person must come to understand and embody in his behavior. Appreciation of the limitations and potentialities in another's value system does not mean the worker adopts it for himself; appreciation of the positives in his own does not mean that he urges it upon others. There were many illustrations in student evaluations of "good" learners which showed the necessity for mastering this aspect of the professional social worker's approach to values. The material from every assisting school stressed the importance of "appreciation of all kinds of persons," and also laid both positive and negative stress on a social worker's self-

22 Gordon Hamilton, "Self-Awareness in Professional Education," *Social Casework,* XXXV, 9 (November, 1954), 371–379.

knowledge of his own values, praising its presence and criticizing indication of any lack. In several class audits, including two at sectarian schools, stress was laid on the delay or defeat of the helping process which could result from a worker's effort to persuade people with whom he was working to follow the worker's sense of values.

OBJECTIVE III:

Awareness [23] of Typical Professional Positions with Respect to Values and Ethics

RELATED KNOWLEDGE

This objective implies familiarity with the whole range of values discussed in Chapter III which will only be summarized here.

In social work literature, in faculty responses to the questionnaire, in discussions with practicing social workers, and in audits of classes the value mentioned most often and given highest significance was that each human being is an object of infinite worth, and as such must be approached with respect and consideration and helped to achieve his own self-maximation. Depending on variations in ultimate value systems, the individual is seen as deserving of the utmost cherishing because of man's infinite untapped possibilities for continually expanding his self-satisfaction and social contribution. (This does not mean that, to be valued, any one individual *must* contribute.) Ideas concerning the mystical origin of man which are part of the basic Judaeo-Christian orientation in our whole culture have resulted in a general conviction that any one living should be treated as befits a representative of this uniquely precious race. Life is precious for under even the most adverse circumstances there might be possibilities for its enrichment. Society must value the individual, and he must value himself and others. The essential idea of social work seems to be that every one of these valuable individual members of mankind should have opportunity to develop, but he cannot do this alone. Social

[23] "Awareness" is a state of being informed and cognizant of the major attributes of a situation or condition. It implies a kind of total intellectual readiness which can be activated and utilized instantaneously. In this context, it implies a more detailed, exhaustive and explicit coverage of content than comprehension.

work sees human living as an on-going process where billions of individuals are giving and taking. Ideally each should be able to take from others at the appropriate time what is required for his optimum self-maximation, and in turn give others all that he could contribute to their development.

On such ultimate ideals concerning a good society of cherished individuals, the rest of the social work value system is built. These include creation of opportunity, self-discovery of personal potentialities, optimum social use of each individual's potentialities. Because of man's infinite possibilities, all of which could never be attained in one individual, social work values variations, as long as there is inner personal satisfaction, a social contribution, and no one else is handicapped by another's self-realization. Social work upholds the rights of people to determine their own affairs and be different. These ideas have been expressed by many social workers, some in articles that have become classic. The new social worker should be familiar with the historical development and gradual evolution of these concepts and with some of the most famous expressions of them. He should also know what the current status is with regard to ethical formulations and be familiar with the content of formulated codes.[24]

APPLICATION IN PROFESSIONAL LIFE

Relation to the Cultural Milieu—Verbalized in this general way, most people in our culture probably might, without much consideration, affirm social work's ultimate value positions. Whatever is unique about social work is probably the persistence and degree of consistency with which these values are sought and implemented in living situations. Social work is continuously striving to find ways to help individuals discover how they may more nearly attain personal fulfillment, and ways they may be helped to band together to create opportunities and remove obstacles for all. Perhaps social work is also distinctive in its disvalues, or in its belief that each value must be sought discriminatingly or consequences regarded as disvalues may ensue, *e.g.*, the use of unbridled free enterprise or competition. Also, social work insists on literally applying values

24 See Appendix E, Classified Bibliography (Descriptions of Social Work Values and Ethics), and listing of proposed minimum content, Chapter VI.

in life areas and among groups which many persons would not include. The words *"every"* individual, *"each"* group, *"all"* people which are found in social work statements may provide a clue to deviations of social work value priorities from those of the general culture. They also provide clues to the type of professional frustration which each social worker must early learn to accept as one of the profession's limitations growing out of its peculiar relation to the total milieu.[25] For example, a student worker was much distressed because fine health facilities not being fully used were not made available to a large sub-culture group. She had to be taught by her field teacher to deal with the conflict between social work's point of view on this and the view of the total community. She was then able to work out a partial relaxation of the restrictions on the use of the facility, which, in turn, she had to be helped to see as progress though it was to her an unsatisfactory compromise.

Social workers have to be alert to values in the culture which do not provide for or actively hinder individual growth, or which oppose a type of society which encourages opportunity for each to contribute. They should understand origins and manifestations of racism, paternalism, social Darwinism with emphasis on preference for the "fit" or "superior," authoritarianism, uncontrolled economic competition. They must see these as large conceptual positions, and also in their specific effects on people.

Relation to Members of the Profession—Commonly held values are the source of motivation for common professional activities and interpersonal cohesiveness. Working together for continued clarification of what social work stands for [26] will tend to minimize the areas of difference between professional sub-groups.

Familiarity with past attempts to describe acceptable profes-

---

[25] Babcock, *op. cit.;* Boehm, "The Role of Values in Social Work," *op. cit.;* Nathan E. Cohen, "Desegregation—A Challenge to the Place of Moral Values in Social Work Education," *Proceedings,* of Third Annual Program Meeting of the Council on Social Work Education, 1955 (New York: Council on Social Work Education, 1955); Grace L. Coyle, "The Social Worker and His Society," *Social Service Review,* XXX, 4 (December, 1956), 387–399; Ginsburg, "The Impact of the Social Worker's Cultural Structure on Social Therapy," *op. cit.*

[26] Student use of such material in a thesis is illustrated in Sophie Jacob Smith, "The New York Times Hundred Neediest Cases: Analysis of the Changes in the Appeals of 1930, 1939, and 1956" (Unpublished Master's project, Graduate School of Public Administration and Social Service, New York University, 1957).

sional behavior motivates current attempts at study of the nature of the profession, and clarifies modes of communication between members of the profession. (See Chapter I on Function of Professional Ethics.) Understanding of what social work ordinarily stands for relieves the worker of part of the burden of constant decision, making completely *de novo* and makes group experience available as a basis of consideration—a pattern of limits and possible goals within which the social worker's judgment can be artistically determined. He can count upon other social workers to behave within certain limits of behavior, and they can count upon him. A good example of this is the professional instrumental value of identity with the purpose of the agency.

Learning experiences should provide some opportunity for identifying this content in concrete situations: points of applicability of ethical norms, places where such values as individual maximation, social responsibility, democratic participation are operative. Examples where social work points of view can be assumed and relied on in colleagues and tested with mutual respect should be included, *e.g.,* that a colleague in another agency might not be free to divulge information obtained within the confidential relationship.

Awareness of typical positions involves an understanding of how they occur in practice, with many variations and often without clear-cut indication of an unquestioned alternative to be selected.

Relation to Clientele—A clearly understood and personally affirmed set of professional values helps the worker to define goals and priorities in all his helping activities, and to determine where limits must be set in encouraging or permitting client activity.[27] It provides a mediating instrument between the demands of the client and society. It helps clarify in what ways social work may be a bearer of values, in what ways a contributor to the reinterpreting of values. The process of preserving, perfecting, and creating institutions which enhance values [28] (*e.g.,* the family, informal educa-

[27] This is illustrated numerous times by Beck, *op. cit.,* and Elliot Studt, "Value Systems and Juvenile Delinquency," in *Group Work and Community Organization Papers* (New York: National Conference of Social Work by Columbia University Press, 1956), 21–29.
[28] Eleanor E. Cockerill *et al., A Conceptual Framework for Social Casework* (2nd ed.; Pittsburgh: University of Pittsburgh Press, 1953), 1–3.

tion) is part of social work practice. (See Objective I for further application to the client-worker situation.)

OBJECTIVE IV:

Ability [29] to Interpret Social Work Positions

RELATED KNOWLEDGE

The social worker's understanding of values in the general culture and social work positions (see Objectives I and III) is the basis on which he can help clarify the content and rationale of social work points of view. He needs to know what aspects of social work convictions are most difficult for the lay person to accept, and the historic and current cultural reasons for this.

Knowledge should include familiarity with instances when social work acts as a culture bearer, or reinforcing mechanism with respect to values, or when it acts as a force for changing values.

APPLICATION IN PROFESSIONAL LIFE

Relation to the Cultural Milieu—An ability to pick out values pervasive in the general culture, identical with or similar to those held by social workers and their clients makes it possible to show boards and sources of financial or political support how social work agencies can implement community goals. Thorough comprehension of value principles assists in helping lay people see the ultimate consequences of proposed decisions in terms of common standards and aspirations. Meaningful interpretation requires ability to relate large values and disvalues to specific issues and situations. The consequences of some popular negative values, as compared with social work's views of its positives, must be made vivid. For instance, the results of punishment and deprivation as instrumental values to attain conformity to social standards, compared with the advantages of increased opportunity for self-expression, often have to be illustrated.

A student discussed "democracy" with an irate community person who objected to a Negro child's participation in group activi-

29 An "ability" is a developed faculty to act consistently in an appropriate or suitable manner.

ties in a partially segregated area, on grounds that democracy should permit local decisions on such matters. The student pointed out that democracy also was often taken to mean equal opportunity and said frankly that conceptions of what might be democratic varied. Although not wholly convinced, the person did not publicly criticize the agency as had been threatened.

Relation to Members of the Profession—A characteristic of every profession is machinery for communicating its meaning to new entrants and sharing its findings among the membership. In the supervisory and teaching relationships social work has to make its value system explicit. Members of the profession working in a variety of specializations, settings and auspices often differ about value positions and ways to apply ethical patterns of behavior. They must be able to interpret their positions to each other if such differences are to be understood and resolved. Beginning with an agreed upon ground of common ultimate values, immediate goals and means for implementation can be arrived at with minimum strain. Similarly, interpretation is needed between different administrative levels. High administrators appeared, in the scanty reports of student experiences, to expect unquestioned acceptance of agency policy and to stress worker responsibility. Field teaching emphasized this and there were fewer examples of the teaching of worker's rights, and the channels through which worker opinions and impressions could be interpreted to administrators. The ability to present a point of view is needed for communication in both directions.

Relation to Clientele—Explanation of agency function requires an ability to make clear what social work tries to do. Understanding of pervasive social work values in the general culture, the client's former and present social values, and agency values assists in the process of setting immediate and long-time goals with the client. If a commonly accepted purpose of social work is to effect change [30]

[30] There is a constant reiteration that "improvement" or "change" to something "better," "more suitable," "more appropriate," "socially acceptable" is a social work goal. *E.g.,* Helen Harris Perlman, *Social Casework* (Chicago: University of Chicago Press, 1957), speaks of "consolidation of constructive desirable change;" Werner A. Lutz, *Concepts and Principles Underlying Social Casework Practice* (Washington, D.C.:

in individuals, groups and communities, it is necessary to show both the direction and goal of change. It is equally important to show clients what social work cannot do, and in which of a client's activities a social worker cannot participate. Understanding social work goals, knowing how other social workers have successfully met ethical problems, helps the social worker utilize limits and opportunities in a professional treatment relationship. The ability to interpret in terms of goals is needed to explain function and methodological approaches of agencies to the clientele, so that they can judge whether agency values coincide with their own. For instance, a worker made clear that it was not the agency's function to decide for a parent that he place a mentally retarded child outside his home. He did explain the agency's concern for the well-being of the total family, including other children, and their concern for the limited child, and concern that the parents feel comfortable in their decision. His interpretations of social work values in these regards, and how they governed his function, activated the clients' appraisal of what values were most important to them.

OBJECTIVE V:

Ability to Withstand Pressures to Change Value Positions and Ethical Judgments

RELATED KNOWLEDGE

Familiarity with the general value system of the profession and the feeling that other social workers would probably take the same position that he does sustains the social worker when he is urged to non-professional conduct. It also prevents his falling victim to the fallacy that what is, is "good."

The social worker needs to be familiar with current and past instances when professional social workers have "held the line" in

National Association of Social Workers, Medical Social Work Section, 1956), of "controlled changes," 1; Gisela Konopka, "Social Work's Search for a Philosophy with Special Reference to Eduard C. Lindeman" (Unpublished doctor's dissertation, The New York School of Social Work, Columbia University, 1957) [To be published by Minnesota Press, 1958], of "improvement of human society," 10; Ackerman, *op. cit.,* of "change in both," (Society and the individual); Florence Hollis, "The Generic and Specific in Social Casework Re-examined," *Social Casework,* XXXVII, 5 (May, 1956), 211–219, "toward a better life."

the face of opposition. Examples might be: the insistence on the abolition of child labor; the support of the social security act; the oppostion to the Jenner amendment; insistence on the validity of cash relief; support of social workers who have been attacked for upholding civil rights of minority groups.

In evaluations of students two qualities described positively might appear, superficially, to be opposed to each other. There is praise for flexibility, willingness to adapt and not insist on one course of action. At the same time there was praise for standing ground when an issue needed to be faced, for not getting stampeded or over-persuaded, for not being unduly influenced by power or prestige, or by effective propaganda or fluent argument. In one community organization class audited, a worker in a case under discussion was approved for not giving in to community pressure to ostracize and force removal of a colored family. In another, positive reference was made to a social worker's refusal to cooperate with a group which wished to change the confidentiality clause in a welfare law, even though members of the political and financial power structure were back of the measure and agency board members were in accord with them. Another maintained the belief a settlement house in a border state should be bi-racial. In developing these objectives, the panel did not feel that "ability to withstand pressure" was in conflict with appreciation of the values of others. This appeared to be an area which, in the author's opinion, needs refining in statements of professional ethics. Nevertheless, in faculty conferences, how to develop the ability to take positions on issues and maintain them even under difficulty or opposition was one of the problems teachers were most concerned about. The question is touched obliquely in social work periodical literature in the insistence that social workers need to contribute their knowledge to reform efforts and that they should enter into social action.[31]

APPLICATION IN PROFESSIONAL LIFE

Relation to the Cultural Milieu—Numerous studies have shown that social workers tend to take value positions at variance with

[31] *E.g.*, Herbert Bisno, "How Social Will Social Work Be?" *Social Work*, I, 2 (April, 1956), 12–18; Gordon Hamilton, "The Role of Social Casework in Social Policy," *Social Casework*, XXXIII, 8 (October, 1952), 316–324.

some of those held by persons in the power structure, and hence the social worker frequently is subject to social, political and economic pressures to modify or abandon his position.) Conviction as to the validity of his values and commitment to them helps the worker accept himself as "being different" in certain respects *because he is a social worker* and aware of professional expectations as to how he will behave. Much of the growing literature on the social worker in social action touches on these points. There is not complete uniformity, but the author gained the impression from audits that teachers at present are encouraging students to feel that as professional people they should learn to take a stand on issues and maintain it on occasion even in the face of opposition from boards and the supporting public.

Relation to Members of the Profession—It is the opinion of the author that a social worker not only tries to follow the recommendations for ethical behavior, but actively supports other workers when they are behaving in an approved ethical manner and under social, political or economic threat, *e.g.,* helping a social group worker find a new position after discharge because of his insistence on hiring of staff irrespective of race. This is not to imply that the content of the curriculum should inculcate automatic or blind support for anything any social worker may do. The positive approach to enforcing professional values is to uphold members and to make sure they are not punished unduly for personal efforts to enforce standards. This implies as well the opposite approach, a willingness to participate if necessary in professional discipline of unethical members. An example of support by the profession is that given to public welfare workers in Indiana when they opposed the bill authorizing anyone to read a welfare record on request. Many social workers, in a great variety of agencies, often with the disapproval of boards and threats from financial backers, protested against the bill and took measures to provide jobs for some who were discharged as a result of their activities.

A few schools have experimented successfully with the case records of NASW support of workers who are attacked while upholding a defined ethical principle. Records showing how workers have withstood community opposition are something included in courses on social work philosophy and current social issues.

A counter opinion was expressed by one faculty member in an audited class, who thought a social worker did not enter in any controversial situation nor support any social action except that directly affecting the work of his own agency. For example, a probation officer would be the only worker justified in protesting poor court conditions; workers in the mental hospital service could work for better hospital legislation, but family agency workers should not. All other class audits and literature examined failed to corroborate this point of view. There were many references to how social workers could support efforts for change affecting agencies with very different focus from their own.

Relation to Clientele—Particularly in community organization and group work, but also with individual clients, the worker may be asked to do something illegal or in violation of a social work tenet, such as "respect for each individual." The feeling of potential support of fellow professionals helps him approach such problems with integrity and consistency. A student was asked by a client for help in securing the services of an abortionist, and replied that he could not ethically collaborate in breaking a law and violating the ethics of another profession. He was reassured that other social workers would have taken the same position.

OBJECTIVE VI:

Recognition [32] of Classic Conflict Positions in a Social Work Situation

RELATED KNOWLEDGE

Historically, because of social work's dual focus on the improvement of individuals or groups and of the communities in which they function, social workers have found themselves facing certain types of value conflicts or ethical problems which are still met repeatedly. Often they are obscured by other concurrent issues or by unique individual aspects, but the worker may be helped to

---

[32] This type of "recognition" implies identification of a situation as similar in certain important characteristics to many previous ones. It is similar to a biologist's recognition that a new specimen belongs to a long identified species.

deal with them by knowing that what is basically involved is one of these fundamental points of difference.

Questions and issues of this kind, such as public versus private sponsorship, the role of social workers in political controversy, the relation of organized religion to social work, belief in upholding civil rights and political freedom, have arisen often in practice. They can be presented in such a way that the student is alerted to their probable occurrence in his practice and to the circumstances in which they are likely to arise.

Examples occurring in audits were: location of final authority between lay boards and professional staff; individual client versus social good; the exercise of authority as against client self-determination; relative responsibility and authority of social work opinion in comparison with other professions; the role of government.

Workers need to be familiar with policy statements of their agency, of professional organizations, and of other organizations dealing with social action in areas touched by social work, in order to sense characteristic thinking and action.

APPLICATION IN PROFESSIONAL LIFE

Relation to the Cultural Milieu—Recognizing that many of these classic situations can occur, in which it may be anticipated that substantial segments of the community will be responding to different values than those held by social workers, it is the worker's responsibility to see that what he is dealing with may have much larger implications than the issues that seem to be at stake in the immediate problem. The range of possible solutions and resources for meeting such a situation becomes much clearer when a familiar syndrome is identified.[33]

[33] Many such classic alternatives are inferred in NASW policy statements, American Association of Social Workers, "Procedures for Considering Complaints of Unethical Conduct of Members" (Approved by the 1953 Delegate Assembly; New York: AASW, #2749, 1953); AASW, *Standards for the Professional Practice of Social Work, op. cit.;* NASW, Delegate Assembly *Workbook I,* Delegate Assembly *Workbook II, op. cit.;* National Association of Social Workers, "Goals of Public Social Policy" (Unpublished draft, 1956); National Association of Social Workers, "Procedures for the Consideration of Complaints Against Agencies for Violations of Social Work Personnel Practices" (Master copy, mimeographed; New York: NASW, #546-23/S). Since the author did not find many illustrations in class sessions of how this material might be presented in syndrome form for recognition and diagnostic usage, this suggestion must be regarded as a theoretical hypothesis by the author concerning how such material might

Relation to Members of the Profession—The basis for much professional cohesion so far has been found in common efforts to determine characteristic and proper professional behavior in problem situations likely to be faced at one time or another by all members, and to interpret this ideal social work behavior to persons outside the profession. The *Standards for the Professional Practice of Social Work* and many statements adopted by workers in professional organizations are largely compilations of situations that have proved indigenous to many settings and methods. The continuous process of identifying causes and areas of activity where social workers consider themselves justified in maintaining a point of view unites and enhances the profession in the eyes of other professions and lay people.

In all such situations the worker must know possible consequences, and his rights and responsibilities as they have emerged in other similar conditions. For example, a student in a public welfare agency was helped to see that the antagonism he encountered personally from a group in the community was part of the long controversy over public versus private auspices. He was interested in seeing how this had worked out at other times and in other places.

Relation to Clientele—As with relations to the general milieu, certain conflicts of values occur again and again. Quick recognition of the value conflict or ethical problem involved, and its syndrome of complicating and associated factors, helps speed diagnosis and insures a consistent behavior in the worker. For example, the problem most frequently mentioned in audits and field work evaluations was that of determining when sacrifice of confidentiality of disclosures might be demanded in the interests of a helpless person or possible threat to the community. Other such problems were how far a small group can be permitted to deviate from accepted legal and moral standards and when belief in equal access to social opportunities could be sacrificed to recognition of limitations in community attitudes.

With respect to the client, "right" seemed to be mentioned

---

function educationally. It should be examined in mature practice before its efficacy is assumed. As a beginning, a faculty curriculum committee might develop a few classic conflicts to be emphasized.

oftener than "duty" or "responsibility." With respect to the worker, "duty" to agency and client was stressed. Each of these can be more validly perceived as a familiar general type of confrontation involving the seeking of a balance between "right" and "duty."

OBJECTIVE VII:

The Ability to Use Professional Procedures and Channels in Resolving Conflicts

RELATED KNOWLEDGE

Two major channels for resolution of differences are available to every worker: first, resources within his agency (such as consultation with colleagues and administrative supervisors, appeal to formal machinery) and second, consultation with and appeal to professional membership organizations.

A worker should be familiar with professional norms as to rights and obligations in his role as society's representative in the giving of help; when and how to consult fellow professionals for further interpretation of rights and obligations; how to participate with other members of the profession in further clarification of professional ethics; how to compromise without jeopardizing ultimate achievement of values by accepting proximate as well as ultimate goals; how to develop positive measures for working with other professionals to achieve change; and how to support other members of the profession when their value judgments are threatened by adverse community attitudes or substandard agency policies.[34]

[34] Some of these problems are touched on in Beck, *op. cit.;* Bisno, "How Social Will Social Work Be?" *op. cit.;* Swithun Bowers, O.M.I., "Human Values and Public Welfare," *The Social Worker,* XXIII (December, 1954), 1–7; Coyle, "The Social Worker and His Society," *op. cit.;* Hamilton, "The Role of Social Casework in Social Policy," *op. cit.;* Margaret Hogan, "Psychiatric Social Work in Mental Hospitals," in *Education for Psychiatric Social Work,* Proceedings of the Dartmouth Conference. (New York: The National Institute for Mental Health, 1949); Florence Hutner, "Professional Responsibility and Leadership Development," *Jewish Social Service Quarterly,* XXX, 3 (Spring, 1954), 239–241; Clara Kaiser, "Social Group Work Practice and Social Responsibility," in *The Social Welfare Forum, 1952* (New York: National Conference of Social Work by Columbia University Press, 1952); Harry L. Lurie, "The Responsibilities of a Socially Oriented Profession," in *New Directions in Social Work* ed. by Cora Kasius (New York: Harper & Brothers, 1954), 31–53; Grace F. Marcus, "The Advance of Social Casework in Its Distinct Social Usefulness," *Social Casework,* XXXVI, 9 (November, 1955), 391–399; NASW, Delegate Assembly *Workbook* I, Delegate As-

This involves general familiarity with publicly accepted pronouncements of NASW and other organizations, and an understanding of how they can be applied in individual situations; examples of personnel practice statements of agencies, civil service machinery in public agencies; administrative theory on personnel obligations, assigned roles, and channels.

An example of professional ethical judgment involving the professional behavior of using proper channels is an ability to determine in questionable situations when a fellow worker is acting in conformance with professional ethics (formulated or unformulated) and when he is not, and what behavior on the part of colleagues is indicated in either case. There is danger of ingrown defense of traditional patterns. There is, in the author's opinion, also the danger that "good" performance based on sound ethical choice may be overlooked, or not supported if stress situations occur.

Students were greatly interested in an edited record of intra-agency and AASW action in a case of alleged professional misconduct which incorporated most of these items. Beyond formal codes, there is, as yet, little written material in this area.[35] Examples of the use of professionally approved channels are needed. These ought to include examples of workers appealing personal grievances, of agencies disapproving worker behavior, of fellow workers and professional associations backing behavior they consider appropriate but which received adverse community criticism.

APPLICATION IN PROFESSIONAL LIFE

Relation to the Cultural Milieu—A professional organization is the characteristic way in which channels are provided for resolving conflicts as a representative of a profession rather than as an independent person. Every worker should be familiar with the ma-

---

sembly *Workbook II, op. cit.;* NASW, "Goals of Public Social Policy," *op. cit.;* Pray, *op. cit.;* Arnold M. Rose, "The Social Responsibility of the Social Scientist," *Social Problems,* I, (January, 1954), 85–90; Louis H. Towley, "Professional Responsibility in a Democracy," in *Education for Social Work,* Proceedings 1953 Annual Program Meeting (New York: Council on Social Work Education, 1953), 10–21; Wayne Vasey, "Public Relations, An Inescapable Obligation in Social Welfare," *Social Service Review,* XXVII, 4 (December, 1953), 394–398.
35 Committees of NASW are now studying the possibility of publishing records of appeals in cases of violation of personnel and ethical standards.

chinery provided for group handling of problems beyond his own understanding or ability to solve, and for the formulation of opinion on how new problems emerging from new demands on the profession may be solved. Evaluations indicated that many schools consider it essential that a student be familiar with the current working of professional organizations, especially NASW but also other such as American Public Welfare Association and National Social Welfare Assembly. In one school where final oral examinations are given, this material was frequently covered in questioning and was a deciding factor in determining readiness for beginning practice.

Relation to Clientele—In planning the helping process in a particular situation the individual practitioner, through his professional organization and his professional history, has models of how conflicts might be resolved. This is the type of knowledge that one would anticipate would emerge from the current NASW study of practice. For the mature worker, it would involve such abilities as how to determine when consultation with experts within and outside the agency was indicated; which decisions could rest with the worker, which must be solved through administrative decisions; when permissible exceptions to usual routine procedures were appropriate. In relation to the clientele, particularly when the "client" is a community or segment of a community, students appeared to be helped by examples of worker behavior which forestalled formal appeal or overt conflict. The author was unable to locate teaching records showing such situations but found teachers recounting them orally. Workers need to have had some vicarious experiences of this sort in order to identify the kind of behavior which is appropriate and acceptable professionally in a threatened or suddenly developing conflict situation. In the author's opinion this is a type of content which the profession and educators should develop in more readily usable form.

OBJECTIVE VIII:

Appreciation of Common Ultimate Goals of Many Branches of the Profession, and Recognition of Unity of Purpose in these Diverse Efforts

This is often referred to in evaluations of students and comments regarding oral examinations as "good identity with the profession as a whole." To the author, "identity" was a too-inclusive ambiguous word which should be broken down into component parts. This objective, as now worded, seemed to be implied in the content of many statements using "identity." Even more specific behavioral manifestations of "identity" would probably develop through concerted faculty observation or workshop effort.

RELATED KNOWLEDGE

A familiarity with the whole social work value system as developed in Chapter III, including its historical derivation and current operational manifestations, plus information about social work institutional structure, is the knowledge base on which is developed feeling of universality [36] in ultimate purpose and pride in the diverse means through which social work implements its values.

The author received the impression that many students develop identity with a particular method or agency and tend to think of it as the "real" or "most important part of" social work. Negatively, a lack of appreciation of other specialties and fields than his own was the second most frequently mentioned short-coming in evaluations. In talks with students, there was a consistent impression of a hierarchy of prestige and importance in different fields. In presenting the value system, the author gained the impression that this tendency was offset when illustrations from many methods and settings were presented *at the same time.* In some field work, other agencies were sometimes presented almost as antagonists who must be won over, or as uninformed or non-understanding.

While the level of social work performance varies greatly, and students early must learn this, it also seemed important that field

[36] See footnote 34 and Classified Bibliography of social work value statements. Too late for inclusion in data analysis, the NASW Statements prepared for Delegate Assembly, 1958 reflect much the same idea in defining the public image of the social worker. NASW, Delegate Assembly *Workbook I, op. cit.,* 24, 29.

instructors, particularly, include a positive picture of other agencies' contributions as well as their handicaps and shortcomings.

APPLICATION IN PROFESSIONAL LIFE

Relation to the Cultural Milieu—It is important in all relations with the public to see social work activity as a whole, to see the contribution of each individual agency, and to assume responsibility for correcting any misunderstandings and for stressing the importance of the work of other agencies as well as our own. When, for instance, a public agency comes under criticism professional people in private agencies can show how the work of that agency is essential to the work of their own. The lay public tends to think of social work in a unitary way, and any public disagreements or failures of mutual support tend to weaken the public appreciation of the profession.

A student in a public recreational agency had been in doubt about the time she had used in discussing the work of a privately sponsored casework agency while she was on a collateral interview with a prominent person, who asked about a financial campaign then going on. As a result of her interpretation a large check was sent to the private agency. The supervisor took conference time to show that the student knew more about the work of the private agency than did an uninformed community person and had a professional responsibility to show that although the two agencies were in different methods and settings they were working from a common philosophy and toward common goals. At the end of her education, the final evaluative statement referred to the exceptionally broad and understanding "identification" with the profession which this student exhibited. One can only speculate as to whether the satisfaction she experienced in the early field experience was in any way related.

Relation to Members of the Profession—One of the recognized handicaps of the profession has been the feeling of caste between specialties and auspices and the lack of unified pride in common components.

If we really believe in respect for all human beings, professional persons dealing with chronic situations with poor prognosis, with people with extreme deviant behavior, or with people with social needs of a less glamorous type should all be seen as serving the same ultimate purpose and be afforded equal recognition in committees and professional organizations.[37]

It is the writer's opinion that possibly social work has not as yet developed sufficient profession-wide identification, nor created a feeling of obligation to uphold social work values and defend fellow members who uphold them under limitations imposed by social and legal customs. This does not mean defense of limited or inadequate performance. It may mean support for limited performance stemming from difficulties beyond the worker's control and efforts to help overcome such difficulties. Students were interested in efforts in one state to back adoption workers who were trying to work toward standards they could as yet not maintain. Students eagerly listened to, and seemed to gain a sense of identification from, accounts of efforts by social workers in many agencies to stand firm in support of public officials opposing abolition of confidentiality laws. They were impressed with federal officials who opposed efforts to reduce public assistance standards. They followed discussions with penetrating questions when stories of political pressure to force resignation or dismissal because of new political alignments were presented. They welcomed accounts of civil servants performing well under pressure, and questioned how professional approval of them could be expressed. In seminars, questions were raised as to how workers in agencies not financed by community chests could support sound positions taken by workers in chest agencies but criticized publicly with threat of discontinued donations.

Students responded to accounts of support by private agencies for legislative measures under consideration and of support of private fund-raising efforts by public agency workers. A rather large literature [38] is developing which appeals to social workers to see

---

[37] Beck, *op. cit.;* J. F. deJongh, "Man's Quest for Freedom and Security: Implication... for Social Work Education in the Twentieth Century." [Presented in the Graduate School of Social Work Seminar, University of Pittsburgh, May 10, 1957.] (Mimeographed). Eveline Burns, "Comments" (typewritten); Furman, *op. cit.;* Elliot Studt, "The Contribution of Correctional Practice to Social Work Theory and Education," *Social Casework,* XXXVII, 6 (June, 1956), 263–269.
[38] Beck, *op. cit.;* Bisno, *op. cit.;* Bowers, "Social Work and Human Problems," *op. cit.;* Cohen, "Desegregation—A Challenge to the Place of Moral Values in Social Work

the immediate concerns of segments of the profession as concerns of the entire professional body. In a number of classes teachers stressed that this concern finds expression both in united social action efforts of professional membership organizations, and in the social worker's personal efforts as a citizen and resident of his own community. While there is not yet, and probably should not be, any fixed formula for a worker's obligation under such circumstances, the present content of advance seminars and NASW releases would suggest that some discussion of such problems should be included in the curriculum content.

Relation to Clientele—In cooperative relationships between agencies, particularly referral and consultation, an attitude of mutual respect and confidence is essential for adequate service to the clientele. Being able to recognize whether differences are about the means to a common goal or the priorities to be accorded to different goals contributes to a helpful working relationship. Many of the explicit ethical recommendations of the profession are based on the assumption that all professional activities are significant. Case material which shows how the work of less glamorous agencies supports the work of others should be part of content. For example, one class in advanced use of group work in therapy was eager to learn more about how community organization efforts were being mobilized to support larger budgets for group therapy in a public convalescent hospital. The teaching of the ethical obligation for mutual support and respect of one part of the profession for another was especially effective when its direct relation to services was thus clarified.

OBJECTIVE IX:

Ability to Use His Own Value System in a Helping Relationship

RELATED KNOWLEDGE

Much has been written about the importance of self-awareness, a major ingredient of which is self-knowledge in relation to the

Education," *op. cit.;* Coyle, "The Social Worker and His Society," *op. cit.;* Lester B. Granger, "Social Work's Response to Democracy's Challenge," in *The Social Welfare Forum, 1952* (New York: The National Conference of Social Work by Columbia University Press, 1952); Hamilton, "The Role of Social Casework in Social Policy," *op. cit.;* Hutner, *op. cit.;* Kaiser, *op. cit.*

worker's own values and his own sense of what is ethical. He must know those things he automatically assumes to be right or wrong and see how these judgments compare with those to be expected from the people with whom he is working. He must know how and at what points his judgments are apt to be exaggerated or dogmatic. He must learn not to expect or require the same responses from others and at the same time to be candid and free in showing that he does have values of his own.[39] There appears to be a larger literature and more material in supervisors' and faculty evaluative statements about the worker's need to be aware of his possible negative reactions (racial and religious attitudes; class reactions as to standards in dress, speech, cleanliness and so on; behavioral manifestations such as disapproval of clients' violent temper) than about his positive ones. This seemed to the author to be one-sided and a somewhat dangerous omission. If social work literature emphatically states that a social worker does his work to produce something "better," it would seem that for planful process, a worker should have a clarified, conscious notion of what he personally considers "good" or "better." From accounts of student supervision the writer was led to the conclusion this was often assumed and not discussed explicitly either in class or field. An exception was found in group work discussion of the hard-to-reach, anti-social natural group.

This whole area is probably one of the most controversial theoretical ones at present. In faculty discussions, some teachers seemed to believe workers should be trained to ignore or by-pass their own values. The author personally doubts this ever is achieved; observation of student response in class and evaluation statements led to the conclusion that personal values play a part in all professional relationships. The objective should be to teach how they can be used positively and consciously, rather than in an unconscious way where they are not subject to conscious controls growing out of awareness.

[39] Estelle Alston, "The Leader's Use of Self," in *Readings in Group Work,* ed. Dorothea Sullivan (New York: Association Press, 1952), 25–38; Cohen, "Desegregation—A Challenge to the Place of Moral Values in Social Work Education," *op. cit.;* Furman, *op. cit.;* Gaynor, *op. cit.;* Goldsmith, *op. cit.;* Sanders, *op. cit.;* Jean M. Snelling, "Professional Leadership in the Social Structure," *Social Casework,* XXXV, 7 (July, 1954), 279–284.

APPLICATION IN PROFESSIONAL LIFE

Relation to the Cultural Milieu—The professional social worker often finds himself in the position of being in a minority in holding certain values. He may judge that in order to achieve their realization he cannot insist on their general application immediately. At the same time, when consulted, it is important that he maintain his own position. A worker in a border city in a group work agency was forthright but not aggressive in stating his belief in non-segregation for staff and clientele. His expression turned out to be an important component in the helping process, setting community members to thinking. One of the ingredients in his helping technique appeared to be his personal integrity in making his point of view known along with his lack of insistence that others hold the same. Somehow, in the content of the curriculum, workers need to gain a sense of how their own values can be expressed and at the same time indicate acceptance but not approval of the different values of others.

Relation to Members of the Profession—In dealing with colleagues in one's own or other agencies, professional ethics demands a respect for their right to their own points of view. This holds true not merely in general interpersonal relationships but also in differences of opinion as to giving service to the clientele.

Students expressed disillusionment concerning lack of acceptance of differing views, and behavior on the part of professional workers which appeared to them to be personal animosity rather than scholarly criticism of divergent positions. Again, part of the learning experience would need to be directed toward learning how personal opinion can be voiced without jeopardizing effective working relations in behalf of the clientele and in the further development of the profession.

Relation to the Clientele—Through self-knowledge of a personally cherished value system the worker is able to help the client discover and apply his own value system. This holds true in working with communities, groups and individuals. A group sometimes places a worker in a position where he is being tested to see if he acts according to the way he believes. The individual client also sometimes asks directly.

In group work with extreme social deviants, it was brought out in several class discussions that part of the helping process involved the group's sensing that the worker liked *them* but could not approve their *behavior,* that this was not merely a professional pose made before them, but that personally the worker would not behave in their way. With individual clients, as well as with community groups, workers have to learn how to indicate their own positions sometimes, and continuously how to be questioning as to whether their own underlying attitudes are entering into the relationship. Some psychiatrists believe it is inevitable that personally held values will color diagnostic opinion and subsequent treatment procedure, so that need for forthright recognition of such factors is considered pertinent and urgent in training.[40] Methods courses and field work seemed to be the most usual places where such content is found at present. Workers need to learn what personal attitudes can appropriately be disclosed to those whom they are helping and which should be withheld. For instance, it might be highly unprofessional for a worker in a public agency to reveal his political preference, but suitable for him to indicate that he could not participate in the planning of gang use of illegal firearms.

In some community organization activities, when directly questioned, a worker decided it was essential that he acknowledge his religious affiliation; in a psychiatric clinic this information might be judged not to be pertinent, nor suitable to know.

OBJECTIVE X:

Use of Common Goals as Motivation for Professional Creativity

The conviction of the extreme importance of achieving professional values acts as a constant urge to discover new ways of accomplishing what the social worker would like to see happen. This should lead to invention of new ways of helping the as yet untreatable social work situations, discovery of new areas of helpful-

[40] See p. 94, for student experience with this type of problem.

ness, willingness to evaluate the success of present endeavors. It helps promote a realistic view of what social work actually is accomplishing.

RELATED KNOWLEDGE

Content to achieve this objective exists in every part of the curriculum—all that is learned concerning the value system and all that is contained in methods courses concerning limitations of present techniques and desirable but as yet unknown knowledge concerning people.

In methods courses and in research courses, the need to know more and the many ways of knowing could be stressed, such as the importance of watching for similarities and differences from which hypotheses can be developed and later tested; the obligation to share experiences in practice when they can contribute to research purposes; the value of small experimentations and the obligation to share results. Studies indicate creativity often stems from the impelling desire to attain values. Students can learn that a desire to attain them is not "unscientific." [41]

APPLICATION IN PROFESSIONAL LIFE

If values serve as a motivating force to spur social workers to inventive creativity, this kind of creativity would find expression in all three areas of professional life: in a drive to more understanding and more ingenious use of values in the general culture, in better organizational machinery for exerting the influence of the profession to achieve values, and in discovery of techniques of service and new areas for their application.

[41] The Bureau of Educational Research, Ohio State University, with which the author corresponded, is working on the hypothesis that values are one of the underlying motivations in creative adult professional life. See Barkan and Mooney, *op. cit.*; Ross L. Mooney, "Cultural Blocks and Creative Possibilities," *Educational Leadership*, XIII (February, 1956), 273–278; Ross L. Mooney, "Evaluating Graduate Education," *Harvard Educational Review*, XXV (Spring, 1955), 85–94.

CONCLUSIONS

GENERAL PRINCIPLES

In order to prepare students able to behave in the essential ways suggested by the objectives, consideration must be given to the present demands of practice, philosophic conceptions of what social work ideally might accomplish, the state of present verbal formulations of values and ethics, the learner as he is met in social work learning. All of the data collected, but particularly student records, faculty opinions, student comments, and isolated successful experiments here and there suggested to the author some very general principles that, until there is more empirically validated experience, might be borne in mind in developing effective learning experiences.

1. *This area of learning can and probably should be planned as fully and carefully as any other* for certain consistent results.

2. *All parts of the curriculum and school experience have potentialities for providing learning experiences.* The contribution of each should be utilized.

3. *The most effective learning appears to occur in groupings of opposites or extremes.* Otherwise there is danger of fragmentation, unequal emphasis and an over-intensive impression of conflicting values and uncertainties.

4. *Social work should be presented as a process of responsible decision-making*—the making of choices between desirable values (particularly the needs of individuals immediately concerned versus the needs of other individuals and larger and more remote groupings, and short-time versus long-time objectives).

5. *Responsibility for introducing each of a minimum list of concepts or central themes to be considered* (to be developed by each faculty group) *should be assigned to a definite place in the total learning system.*

6. *A progression in this type of learning is possible,* geared to stages in student growth.

7. *Learning experiences of three kinds must be provided for,* "atmosphere," formal course instruction, and field experience.

8. *Principles and their application in practice situations must be presented together.* Planned reinforcement of learning between segments of the curriculum is desirable.

MINIMUM CONTENT FORMULATIONS

A suggestion as to the kind of minimum content which might be developed by curriculum committees was assembled by asking faculty members in the schools visited, and in the questionnaires, what had been found most useful. The panel also worked on content possibilities. The following types of material were most often mentioned, and seem to the author to bear direct relation to the objectives:

The nature of values in human experience.[1]

Professional uses of values (worker's own, client's, general society's in the helping process.[2]

[1] Some of this material is contained in the following bibliographical references; Bidney, *op. cit.;* Boehm, "Social Work and the Social Sciences," *op. cit.;* Boulding, *op. cit.;* Lyman Bryson and Louis Finkelstein (eds.), *Science, Philosophy and Religion,* Third Symposium [on Meaning of Values] (New York: Conference on Science and Religion, 1943), Editorial Introduction, 3–7; deJongh, "Man's Quest for Freedom and Security: Implications for Social Work Education in the Twentieth Century," *op. cit.;* Hartman, *op. cit.;* George A. Lundberg, "Can Science Validate Ethics?" *Bulletin of the American Association of University Professors,* XXXVI (1950), 261–275; Jacques Maritain (ed.), *Human Rights, Comments and Interpretations* (A symposium sponsored by the United Nations Educational, Scientific and Cultural Organization; New York: Columbia University Press, 1949); Morris, *op. cit.;* Myrdal, *op. cit.;* Palter, *op. cit.;* Parsons, *Religious Perspective of College Teaching in Sociology Social Psychology, op. cit.;* Parsons, Shils, and Olds, "Values, Motives, and Systems of Action," in *Toward a General Theory of Action,* ed. Parsons and Shils, *op. cit.;* Perry, *Realms of Value, op. cit.;* Pratt, *op. cit.;* Reiser, *op. cit.;* Roshwald, *op. cit.;* Mary J. Shaw, "Social Valuation," in *Modern American Society,* ed. Kingsley Davis, Harry C. Bredemeier and Marion J. Levy (New York: Rinehart, 1949); Leo W. Simmons and Harold Wolff, *Social Science in Medicine* (New York: Russell Sage Foundation, 1954); George Simpson, "Some Problems for Social Philosophy," *Bulletin of the American Association of University Professors,* XXXVI (1950), 516–524; Williams, "Religion, Value Orientations, and Intergroup Conflict," *op. cit.*

[2] Examples of such uses are discussed in: Biestek, "The Non-Judgmental Attitude," *op. cit.;* Biestek, "Religion and Social Casework," *op. cit.;* "Focus on the Multi-Problem Family," *Youth Board News* (May, 1957), 3; Furman, *op. cit.;* Ginsburg, "The Impact of the Social Worker's Cultural Structure on Social Therapy," *op. cit.;* Ginsburg, "Values and the Psychiatrist," *op. cit.;* Hyman Grossbard, "Methodology for Developing Self-Awareness," *Social Casework,* XXXV, 9 (November, 1954), 380–386;

Commonly expressed ultimate social work values.[3]

Middle range abstractions and operational values.[4]

The nature and process involved in ethical choices, *e.g.*, weighs individual good versus good of others; immediate versus long-time goals; professional versus personal types of acceptable behavior; social and individual material and emotional costs of attaining values.[5]

The current state of professionally established ethical norms—codes and descriptions of "good" practice which are in common use.

Professional channels for implementation of values; professional organizations and agency lines of authority.

Classic social work value and ethical involvements and conflicts (see Objective VI).

Most quoted value and ethical pronouncements in social work literature.[6]

Hamilton, "Self-Awareness in Professional Education," *op. cit.;* Ada Kozier, "Casework with Parents of Children Born with Severe Brain Defects," *Social Casework,* XXXVIII, 4 (April, 1957), 183–189; Mary J. McCormick, *Diagnostic Casework in the Thomistic Pattern* (New York: Columbia University Press, 1954); McKenney, *op. cit.;* Helen Padula, "Some Thoughts About the Culture of Social Work," *Journal of Psychiatric Social Work,* XXIII, 4 (April, 1954), 172–176; John R. Reid, "The Problem of Values in Psychoanalysis," *American Journal of Psychoanalysis,* XV, 2 (1955), 115–122; Bernard Warach, "Social Group Work and Sectarian Purpose" (Unpublished mimeographed manuscript, Doctoral Seminar in Social Group Work, New York School of Social Work, Columbia University, 1955).

3 See Classified Bibliography, Descriptions of Social Work Values and Ethics.

4 This is not developed in detail in much of the literature, and is an area for further research. An example would be Martha Eliot, "The Family Today: Its Needs and Opportunities," *Social Casework,* XXIV, 2 (February, 1953), 47–54, for the "good family."

5 Churchman, *op. cit.;* Edel, *op. cit.;* Feigl, *op. cit.;* Robert M. MacIver (ed.), *Conflict of Loyalties* (New York: The Institute for Religious and Social Studies, Harper & Brothers, Distributors, 1952); McGreal, *op. cit.*

6 For a full list of professional value material, see Classified Bibliography. The items the author found most frequently assigned were: AASW, "Procedures for Considering Complaints of Unethical Conduct of Members," *op. cit.;* AASW, *Standards for the Professional Practice of Social Work, op. cit.;* "Code of the Chest and Council Movement," *Community* (April, 1953), 160 ff; Terence J. Cooke, "The Group Members and the Group Work Process in the Light of Thomistic Philosophy," in *Readings in Group Work,* ed. Dorothea Sullivan (New York: Association Press, 1952), 160–178; L. K. Hall, *op. cit.;* Hamilton, "Helping People—The Growth of a Profession," *op. cit.;* Eduard C. Lindeman, "Democracy and Social Work," in *Proceedings of the National Conference of Social Work, 1948* (New York: Columbia University Press, 1948), 79–88; Donald S. Howard, "The Common Core of Social Work in Different Countries," *Social Work Journal,* XXXII, 4 (October, 1951), 163–171; Leonard W. Mayo, "Basic Issues in Social Work," *Proceedings of the National Conference of Social Work, 1948* (New York: Columbia University Press, 1949), 12–30; Herbert Bisno, *The Philosophy of Social Work* (Washington, D.C.: The Public Affairs Press, 1952); Biestek, "The Non-Judgmental Attitude," *op. cit.;* Roy, *op. cit.;* Donald Young, "Sociology and the Practicing Professions."

Ethical norms in other literature which clarify the nature of values held in general, or their relation to social work.[7]

Each curriculum planning committee will have to judge how best these objectives and the minimum core content can be divided into formal courses and field instruction.

A tentative example of possible organization of curriculum by which this might be accomplished is contained in Appendix I.

NEXT STEPS FOR EDUCATION IN VALUES AND ETHICS

Perhaps the chief result of this project may be some sense of the magnitude of the problem, and of the need for much more intensive research as well as greatly accelerated group thinking and experimentation. Each area of exploration was barely touched, compared to what might be produced with more time and increased facilities. Some of the lines along which further, more detailed examination should be pursued are:

1. Better definition of values and major ethical principles, both in terms of what values *actually operate* in guiding practice, and of varying levels of abstraction.

2. Forthright recognition that social workers visualize ends or goals toward which they hope the people with whom they work might move. Use of "change," "growth," "betterment," "general welfare" implies this.

3. Experimentation with different kinds of learning devices, such as teaching in constellations, stress on alternatives, teaching intermediate goals, deliberate use of atmosphere.

4. Production of teaching materials.

We need records from all methods which illustrate the influence of value assumptions and implied goals, consideration of already exist-

[7] Examples of such material are: *Universal Declarations of Human Rights,* United Nations, 1948; *To Secure These Rights,* United States Government Printing Office, 1947; and *Human Rights, Comments and Interpretations.* See also Maritain, *op. cit.;* Williams, "Religion, Value Orientations, and Intergroup Conflict," *op. cit.;* Florence Rockwood Kluckhohn, "Cultural Factors in Social Work Practice and Education," *Social Service Review,* XXV, 1 (March, 1951), 38–47.

ing cultural and spiritual values, how clients acquire values, the interaction of community and professional values.

We need material showing how the profession operates in a unitary way—records of support for workers who behaved ethically and utilized values positively, records of disciplinary action and the consequence of unethical behavior.

We need records which show the worker's professional self-awareness in the handling of his own values.

We need more summarized and adapted social science materials to show how values are acquired and operate—the relation of culture and internal personality.

This is a very large assignment, and one that will be increased in breadth as teachers discover many more potentialities for making values and ethics part of professional preparation.

Suggested Curriculum Organization

Although the object of this project, in conformance with the plan of the entire Curriculum Study, was to formulate educational objectives to be achieved, the experiences reported by faculty members, records of student progress, and content analysis of course outlines and professional literature, seemed to the author to point out some possibilities for an approach to the next step of curriculum organization and devising learning experiences to achieve these objectives. They have been tentatively assembled not as recommendations but as suggestive of one way in which a curriculum committee might set about the task of including values and ethics in the curriculum.

ALLOCATING RESPONSIBILITY FOR A SINGLE CORE

From student and faculty references to specific courses and from observation of student response in class audits, value learning seemed to take place most readily in courses which combined a high level of abstraction with discussion of minute ramifications in specific social work decision-making. Students particularly liked courses where all methods were represented in student and teacher experience and where a principle or a large concept, such as the associated and interacting values of self-determination and individual responsibility for the common welfare, could be weighed at the same time. Students appeared most likely to gain a sense that social work practices what it intellectually affirms when each concept was seen as it worked out or had to be applied, in cases of individual persons, families, intimate groups, community and nations.

Without necessarily organizing an additional sequence for teaching values and ethics, generically focused curriculum courses might be timed in such a way that in each semester one course, at least, cuts across lines of specialization and offers opportunity for relating broad value concepts to varied application. This plan would partially allow for differences in the degree to which different values had been integrated in each student. It could be designed to provide educational experiences particularly suited to the typical stages in student learning, especially if such courses were conducted in classes small enough to offer opportunity for free discussion. Such courses might be as follows:

INTRODUCTORY COURSES IN SOCIAL WORK METHOD
AND ITS PHILOSOPHIC BASE [1]

Taking advantage of the period of initial student enthusiasm for being a part of a profession, during a special orientation period or during early weeks of formal courses, it seemed to be helpful to present social work values at a high level of abstraction, as large goals toward which the entire profession hoped to move *provided* the concepts of partializing and selection of immediate and realistically obtainable goals were presented at the same time, with ample illustrative material from mature practice.

Introduced as large philosophic concepts in the beginning of their education without concurrent practice illustrations, students thought values had little meaning for them. They seemed like ideas everyone takes for granted. "Why belabor that the individual is important or that democracy is a good way of life?" one suggested. This student thought all specific social work methods should have been discussed with each concept, and that it slowed his progress to have to put method and philosophy together on his own initiative. He was enthused over a fourth semester seminar course, and thought a somewhat similar, but less involved course in the introductory stage would have helped him.

Presented as the common foundation of common elements in methodology, professional values were enthusiastically considered by students whose focus in the first semester is primarily on obtain-

[1] Arthur C. Abrahamson, "Formulating a Basic Methods Course," *The Social Worker*, XXV, 1 (October, 1956), 3–8; Hollis, *op. cit.*; Alice B. Hyde and Jeane Murphy, "An Experiment in Integrative Learning," *Social Service Review*, XXIX, 4 (December, 1955), 358–371; Gisela Konopka, "The Generic and Specific in Group Work Practice in the Psychiatric Setting," *Social Work*, I, 1 (January, 1956), 72–80.

ing equipment for their individual field tasks. In schools where field instruction proceeds concurrently from the beginning, class presentation of field material was effectively used in courses on generic method to illustrate major concepts, such as the role of worker and agency in acting as society's representatives to express group concern for the individual. However, in the first semester most students in their desire for a quick professional identification responded most favorably to examples of experienced practitioners' behavior, supplemented with student experience. To conserve time, and to secure comprehensive as well as detailed orientation, a whole case or a full history of a group or community development did not necessarily have to be used; sometimes several crucial incidents from different methods, in which value or ethical choices had to be made, with summary of the outcomes, could serve to show how the social worker's commitment to a value helped him determine a professional course of action. To give the idea that ultimate achievement of goals usually takes place over a long time span, one teacher effectively combined an historical illustration with examples of current practice from each of three social work methods in discussing the importance of client participation in treatment planning.

As a final summary of common aspects of methods and their related value-based concepts, one of the classes audited was studying in detail a record in which different agencies using all three methods contributed to the realization for a family and its neighborhood of many values which had been discussed throughout the course. Final papers required further illustration from the students' own practice, forcing the students to associate abstractions and concrete application.

Such an initial presentation of large objectives, coupled with detailed illustrations from many settings and all the major methods, seemed to be an effective safeguard against early or violent onset of disillusionment arising from fragmentary perception of the meaning of the profession. Although, doubtless, much may be "heard" without full incorporation in practice at this early point, such a course focused on common methodology has the advantage of making the students' initial introduction to underlying philosophy come as applied philosophy of a total profession rather than as a philosophy of one method alone. Students who had taken a somewhat similar type of course spoke of their early pride in all facets of the profession. One recalled, "I was not as much worried as other students in our field agency (where units from several schools were represented) about whether all we were doing was just helping people be satisfied with their lot. I knew that over in another part of the city, other social workers were interesting the same kind of folks in doing something about it, while I was helping the people who were extra unhappy about it, become more able to cope with it *now*." The author is aware that there is much debate over whether method should be introduced in a "common methods" course, but whatever advantages or disadvantages such a course may have in a methods sequence, with respect to values and ethics, something of the sort appeared to be fundamental to further learning.

Tying professionally cherished values to familiar value ideas has the educational advantage of showing immediate respect for the student's self as it has already been developed. In such introductory methods courses, philosophically oriented, the student at once learns he is not being required to change his former value orientations but to expand their usefulness in professional service to others.

Abstract presentations are then not "belaboring" the obvious but, with new illustrations of application, are old familiar ideas made into realistic instead of intangible ideals. Sectarian schools have made positive use of this educational device with respect to long-affirmed religious values, and the same methods might apply generally to familiar political and social convictions. Social work can be presented as providing new opportunities for additional understanding and wider use of already known principles, as well as illustrating their applicability in new situations. For example, "individual responsibility for the common good" was introduced in a first semester class as it applied to provisions for the aged, and it was shown that casework, group work, and community organization each had ways of stimulating such a sense of responsibility in people and helping them learn how to exercise it. "Respect for the infinite worth of each human person" was similarly illustrated in each method in another introductory session. "Dignity" of the individual seems to have most meaning when manifold ways in which a practicing social worker can enhance it are described, and perhaps by showing consequences when individual dignity has not been truly respected in the culture at large.

In such an early introduction to the specific operation of all social work methods as implementation of philosophically affirmed value concepts, some teachers successfully offered the NASW ethical code, explaining it was available as a general guide for the individual social worker in his effort to apply broad principles consistently. A code seemed to serve as a tangible symbol that a unified profession existed. In his last semester one excellent student recalled having read it with awe during his first month in school, wondering how he, personally, could ever make it effective. He dated his feeling of really wanting to become a professional person from his introduction to the code. However, he regretted it had been introduced to him by a teacher in his special method, for it was some time before he realized it was equally applicable in others. He thought it first belonged in some generic course, with frequent later reference to it in specialized methods courses. Offered as one means of achieving professional goals, ethical principles are seen as an integral part of all method, not as a thing apart from everyday practice.

A first semester student wrote "The Code of Ethics . . . proved to be of more concrete help to me than anything else I have read this semester. I used it as an evaluative tool for myself, and considered where I need to grow." Several teachers expressed like opinions from their talks with students.

Without such a course, much of the first semester in each method has to be devoted to introducing value concepts not unique to that method but fundamental to its understanding, and a fragmented professional identification may result.

THE INSTITUTIONAL STRUCTURE OF SOCIAL WORK

Following such an introductory course where methods and their related values are presented together rather than serially, with much moving back and forth between specific situations and large value concepts, the basic course in the social services presenting the institutional structure within which social work operates seemed to take on additional meaning. Students who took the two concurrently spoke of opposite difficulties when some thought it hard to see how the details of organization were consistent with high level value abstractions; others believed that two such courses seemed to duplicate each other. Following a rounded presentation of *what* the profession tried to do and *how* (goals and method), the social services could be presented as society's way of making values operative. Students who believed their most effective learning of values had come in a social services course had had the course following a philosophy, "basic concepts," "introductory method," or ethics course.

During the second semester in most schools each student is taking an intensive course in his own method. The comprehensive course in the institutional aspects of social work at that point offered a means of exchange for students in all methods on the many implementations of values, and was especially significant in helping the student achieve balanced comprehension of social work's focus on both individual and societal needs. When such a course was offered in the second semester, there seemed to be somewhat less frustration that social work had turned out to be different than expected, for many different expectations were illustrated. Discussion of social action, as well as individual and group treatment components in social work, vicariously satisfied some students' need to "do something" about conditions which they could do little about in their field placements.

THE HISTORY OF SOCIAL WORK

Further opportunity to see values in relation to professional activity as a whole can be given by a course in the third semester on the historic development of social work,[2] followed by a seminar in the profession's present, its current issues and trends, and their philosophic implications. Prepared by some understanding of the common aspects of social work methods and by study of its institutional aspects, together with courses in psychological, cultural and physical development of people and in detailed application of one particular method, the third semester student has a fairly rounded picture of what now exists in social work. He is ready to

2 deSchweinitz, *op. cit.*; Arlien Johnson, *op. cit.*

consider how this has come about, to look at values the profession has modified or outgrown, and to see varying attempts at their implementation. History, placed earlier in the curriculum, runs the dangers of duplicating parts of the introductory social services courses and of seeming to teach negatively the things the profession no longer affirms.

By the third semester, the student is ready to see the long-time social process involved in formulating and achieving social goals. The profession itself, as a value, is better understood because of the intimate experience the student has had with it. The advent of the profession, as such, and its gradually emerging ethical formulations can be presented as distillation of professional group experience—a heritage with which the new practitioner can begin and which he can make effective, enlarge and perfect through his own performance. "The profession" as an instrumental value in its own right begins to emerge. Social work's long-continued relation to values in the culture at large and the interaction between the professional culture and conditions of the time offer opportunities to see values in their cultural and time perspectives. The same value may find expression in different ways. The same institutional means may be modified when values change.

One teacher illustrated such a change by showing that child placement might once have been a means of destroying a "bad" family and might now be seen as a means of eventually reconstructing and uniting a "good" one. In three different audits the changing focuses on social work as "cause" and as "function" were discussed, each teacher attempting to relate professional effort to long-accepted values, and also to changing ways of attaining values. Two students spoke of the history course as being the means by which they began to overcome feelings of futility and disillusionment. "Things do get done if you keep working at them," one commented. Values were appreciated and prized when efforts to defend them were studied or the long range consequences of opposing values measured. The achievement of goals over a long time span rather than in a few months of field work helped one field student to place the work he was doing with prisoners in perspective and to accept slow individual growth and limited public understanding. Where history was taught as vicarious experimentations with value application, and with encouragement to make constant comparisons with current conditions and issues as either similar or different value manifestations, the student discovered a new area where abstractions could be linked to their application in reality.

SEMINAR ON THE PROFESSION

Of all courses that happened to be discussed with students, fourth semester professional seminars were most consistently praised. Teachers, also tended to feel such courses were essential in helping round the total learning experience into a cohesive whole, and in completing the process of a student's identification of himself as a practicing member of an esteemed profession. Such courses seemed to fill the need for reassurance during the period of panic at the thought of mature acceptance of full responsibility as a trained practitioner. Students were particularly enthused when the teacher of a seminar came from a different practice background from their own, though this hardly could be feasible curriculum policy in most schools, especially since the learning advantages of mixing student specialties was even more apparent.

In this course conceptualization of values can be seen at all levels: grand or ultimate objectives with which all of society might agree in the abstract; immediate objectives and instrumental means set up or to be created for their attainment; conflict of several values, all affirmed abstractly; the weighing of what kind of personal behavior best exemplified professional values. Behavior can be discussed in terms of specific field problems, current experiments, alternatives other social workers are confronting. A number of teachers found that comparison of the various social work ethical statements so far formulated with those of some other profession was a helpful learning experience for seeking professional identity. One seminar discussed varying ethical commitments to the importance of preserving family units, especially contrasting the psychiatrist and the social caseworker, and the policeman and probation caseworker. Unwritten as well as codified professional usages were often discussed.

Students in the fourth semester are sufficiently mature that examples of unethical behavior, poor personnel practices, violations of civil rights, and so on, can be examined, and professional channels for self-discipline and raising of standards can be studied in detail. One school used a record of an NASW handling of a code violation, and a number of students eagerly reported how much they had learned, corroborating faculty impressions of the success of the experiment. One of the drawbacks of such a course, if wholly unstructured, is that students may place disproportionate emphasis on points of current uncertainties or conflicts rather than areas where professional thinking is fairly solidified and expectations quite definite. For example, the frequent reiteration in audited classes of the present social worker's concern for status was not always balanced by appraisal of present status compared to earlier periods, or by perspective on the uncertain status of other occupational groups. Forces in contemporary society which threaten social work were sometimes cited without equal emphasis on forces which social work can count upon for reinforcing social work objectives.

Seminars seemed most effective when some rounded picture of the profession as presently constituted was attempted, including settled and unsettled points of view, linking of methods to goals, discussing both agency and practitioner obligations. The order and mode of approach was effectively left to student determination; totality of coverage was a faculty responsibility.

SUMMARY

In organizing curriculum to provide specifically allocated responsibility for presenting a core content of value concepts and major ethical expectations, it appears best to this author that they be incorporated in generic courses from other sequences, courses dealing with material regarding the nature of the profession as a whole. Such courses ought to be distributed throughout the four semesters: (1) The Value Base of Social Work Methods, (2) The Present Institutional Structure of Social Work, (3) The Historic Development of Social Work, including enlargement and redefinition of goals and creation of institutions to attain them, (4) The Profession, as seen in personal social work behavior, current issues, and professional decision-making. The profession *per se* becomes a cherished value in such a course.

REINFORCEMENT IN OTHER SEQUENCES OF THE VALUE CORE COURSES

In considering contributions to the teaching of values and ethics which each part of the curriculum may have special ability to develop, the following outline emerged from faculty discussions, audits, and study of curriculum materials. Again, it is presented here as an example of the kind of structure a faculty might build for reinforcement and enrichment of learning, and not in any sense as a complete blueprint.

HUMAN GROWTH AND BEHAVIOR:
The process of value formation; types of value formation; dynamic uses of values.

THE SOCIAL SERVICES:
Institutional means of implementing values; social process in the changing of values and mode of implementation; professional organization as a way of attaining goals held in common; ethical and value formulations so far developed; issues and uncertainties.

CASEWORK METHOD:
Diagnostic practice in determining the degree of internalization of values and possibility of helping a client modify his values; recognition of the influence of worker's values in relationships; identification of value components described theoretically elsewhere in the curriculum; identification of ethical obligations and expectations—what a worker "must" or "should" do; practice in weighing choice between values to be achieved; use of resources which help client to achieve his own values; study of worker's use of his own value system to help client understand and use his own (neither denial nor imposition); study of the role of values in determining treatment goals and focus and in selecting level of treatment and treatment techniques.

GROUP WORK METHOD:
Balance of needs of individual and others; use of personal values in helping; meaning of

"democracy" in action; appreciation of the interaction of sub-cultures with general culture.

THE COMMUNITY
ORGANIZATION METHOD: Implementation of social goals; "starting where the community is;" relation of social work values to community values.

RESEARCH: Relation of insight and speculation to empirically validated values; need for motivation to discover new skills; better definition of social work values.

ADMINISTRATION: The "good agency" and the "good employe" as operational values.

FIELD PRACTICE: Testing the student's level of value formation and learning patterns; practice in identifying values in operation; exposure to values not previously experienced, at least in the same form.

Questionnaire for Project on Values and Ethics

The following questions may be answered by any method that seems best—faculty committee, assignment of sections to different faculty members, circularizing, and so on.

Use additional sheets for reply when necessary.

Since the project must be completed this spring, it is particularly important to have replies to this questionnaire by February 25 if at all possible.

I. Has your school given a course or section of a course in professional ethics *as such* during the last five years?

   Yes ☐ If now in the curriculum, are there teaching notes or committee minutes which indicate faculty reasoning for developing such a course? Describe briefly, or attach the material itself if you prefer.

   If not now in the curriculum, what was faculty reasoning for taking it out?

   No ☐ Has any thought been given to the possibility of such a course? Explain.

II. In what courses do you present major social work goals?

   What goals are stressed most frequently?

III. What ethical principles or social work value commitments would you consider involved in the work situations exemplified below? In what courses would your students be most likely to learn how to handle themselves in such circumstances?

   A. The interests of a client or group being worked with directly seem to conflict with the interests of other persons in the immediate situation, *e.g.,* the needs of the client's absent marital partner; the needs of a child which the mother, your client, fails to see; the rights of a law-abiding neighborhood group on which a teenage group, your group, in a settlement is preparing to wage war.

   B. Agency policies which worker feels do not exemplify usually accepted social work norms, *e.g.,* a segregated community agency.

   C. Personal convictions of worker conflict with the values and standards of conduct of board members or supporting public, *e.g.,* worker believes in trade unions, board does not.

D. A client has applied to two agencies. Each feels it can be of service but believes only one can successfully treat the client.

E. In casework treatment of a marital problem, one partner wants help in securing a divorce; the other is opposed to divorce and wants help in reestablishing the family.

F. A social worker is discharged for refusing to reveal to the court information secured in casework interview concerning a bigamous family.

G. A newspaper urges discharge of a worker who recommended an old age assistance grant for a man known to have been a Communist.

H. A worker and supervisor differ over whether a child should be removed from a "questionable" home situation.

I. A social worker refuses to take a loyalty oath newly required by law for public agency personnel, on grounds of being forbidden by membership in a religious sect.

J. An ADC recipient, mother of six children, has a larger income based on budget than that of her neighbor, fully employed. The Board of the County Department of Welfare is urging grant be reduced, on complaint of neighbor.

K. On the basis of observations of the patient at home, a social worker in a clinic disagrees with medical opinion that the patient is unable to undertake work or training that involves independent travel.

L. Teachers in school and a local minister complain when a social agency helps an unmarried mother and her two children to move into their neighborhood.

Have any similar situations or problems been brought up recently in class or field work? Describe briefly on back of page, under the following headings:

How presented (by teacher as illustration, by case record, by student question)? How handled (student answer, teacher answer, reference to literature)? Did answers lead to generalization of ethical principles? If so, what ones? Was the "usual" social work position as to values or ethics clear? In doubt?

IV. What elements in the general atmosphere of your school do you think contribute to a student's sensing the accepted values of social work? (The following examples are intended to be suggestive but not to limit your thinking:—excused time for special religious holidays, unsegregated dining halls, democratic process in student organization, student participation in national associations and in social action campaigns, protected use of case records, and so on.

V. Where in the curriculum are the following discussed, if at all? Describe briefly.

Civil Rights.

Basic beliefs of the three major religious groups.

Social class differences.

Economic philosophies, such as "welfare state" and "capitalism."

Political philosophies, such as "democracy," "totalitarianism," "state socialism."

Current political events.

Standards of personnel practices.

Cost of living.

Social work salaries.

Violation of professional ethics.

Principles of "prevention" versus "cure."

VI. Of published case records, which ones do you find useful to illustrate the part the social worker's standards of personal and professional behavior must play?

VII. Are any of the following materials assigned as required reading? If so, in what courses?

American Association of Social Workers:

Standards for the Professional Practice of Social Work

Policies and Procedures for Considering Complaints of Unethical Conduct of Members

Personnel Practices Code

U. S. President's Committee on Civil Rights: *To Secure These Rights*

Universal Declaration of Human Rights Proclaimed by the United Nations

Other codes for professional behavior: (specify)

Can you suggest any recent theses in which issues of ethical behavior or professional values have been touched on? List below. Selections may be ordered later on library loan.

Please attach for return with this questionnaire any reading lists, not in course outlines, drawn up for special seminars that deal with the nature and definition of social work, professional obligations, participation in professional organizations.

Compilation of Answers to One Item in the Questionnaire

III. What ethical principles or social work commitments would you consider involved in the work situation below?
   A. The interests of a client or group being worked with directly seem to conflict with the interests of other persons in the immediate situation.

   (Seventy-one separate statements were made. Those with similar or identical phraseology have been grouped. All are direct quotations.)

VALUE COMMITMENTS

   1. Concern for the whole society as well as any segment.
      Common good takes precedence over particular good.
   Society morally justified in demanding that individual serve and subordinate himself up to a point; society ultimately exists to serve individual; the two are correlative.
   2. Individual and group right to conduct lives independently within their personal capacities so long as their actions do not conflict with needs and rights of others.
      Self-determination limited by needs of others and public policy.
      Limitations are part of reality.
      All individuals and groups are alike and all different; common needs of all must be considered; differences must be accepted and provided for.
   3. People individually and in groups have both rights and social obligations.
   4. Belief in people's capacity for improvement.
   5. Forces should be combined for client's benefit.

SOCIAL WORK OBLIGATIONS AND ETHICAL PRINCIPLES

   1. Concern both for client and all others in situation—responsibility to total group and society. (Every answer expressed this in some manner.)

Methods and goals must be considered with respect to needs and rights of all affected.

Clarify who is client.

2. Obligation to use professional knowledge to assess client's (i, g, c) capacities and motivations (degree of ego impairment; basis of community conflict; asocial nature of group norms; destructive mechanisms; determine underlying issues and why conflict with others).

   Obligation to consider cultural as well as personal differences.

3. Obligation to intervene to prevent injury and protect innocent or weak.

   (A number said first obligation was to a helpless child.)

4. Obligation to help client (i, g, c) see his responsibilities as well as rights and desires. Accept individuals and groups but not necessarily their behavior.

5. Responsibility to relate to social structure as a whole, to support affirmative community values to enable each individual and group to function constructively.

   Be a bearer of social values.

   Responsibility to maintain social and legal sanctions—conform to public policy—support law-abiding groups.

6. Obligation to strengthen capacities of individuals, groups, families, communities.

7. Maintain and confidentiality.

8. Professionally discipline own identifications. Consider own personal integrity.

COURSES IN WHICH STUDENTS ARE MOST LIKELY TO LEARN HOW TO HANDLE THEMSELVES. (IN ORDER OF FREQUENCY OF MENTION.)

Introductory Methods: Casework, Group Work, Community Organization.

Field Practice

Advanced Methods

Philosophy, Ethics, Basic Concepts, Seminar in the Profession

Social Services: Social Welfare Organization, Income Maintenance, Social Work in Public Health, Policies and Problems.

Administration

Supervision

Human Growth and Behavior
Research

Examples of Similar Situations Occurring in Class
or Field Discussion

Psychotic patient (his needs and family needs).

Delinquent in a correctional setting.

Worker overidentified with child and unable to see teacher's obligation to others in classroom.

Refusal of mother to permit absent father to visit.

Group Worker expected to teach high moral standards to group with other values who come for "fun."

Client not living with wife but receiving allowance as head of a family group.

Case of tuberculosis person who did not want legally prescribed hospitalization, but endangered family.

List of Words Encountered in Questionnaires, Social Work Literature, and Audits to Express or Convey Value and Ethical Meaning

WORDS REPRESENTING POSITIVE VALUES

Absolute
Accept
Access (to opportunity)
Accountability
Achieve
Adequate
Adjustment
Advantage
Aim
Appreciate
Appropriate
Approved
Aspire
Aspiration
Attending to
Augment

Belief in
Best
Better
Brotherhood
Brotherly

Change
Choice
Chosen
Civil liberty
Collaborative
Commitment
Common good

Concern
Confidentiality
Conscience (of the community, profession, person)
Constructive
Cooperation
Creative

Decency
Democratic
Desirable
Developed
Devoted to development of (capacities to)
Differences (belief in)
Dignity
Discriminating
Duty

Educational
Effective
Empathy
End
Enhance
Equality
Equilibrium
Ethical

Facilitating
Fairness

Faith (in people)
Flexibility
Foster
Freedom
Fulfill
Fulfillment
Furthering (happiness)

Goal
Growth

Happiness
Harmonious
Healing
Health
Healthy

Ideal
Idealize
Impact (create __ upon)
Improving
Indispensable
Individualization
Integrity
Intelligent
Interdependent
Interest
Interrelated

Just
Justice

Kind
Kindness

Limits
Loyal to

Maturity
Means
Mobilization

Mobilize
Modify
Moral
Motivation
Must

Norm
Normalcy

Obligation
Optimum (productive well being)
Ought

Partial
Participation
Perfect
Perfectibility
Permissive
Pity
Pluralism
Positive
Preferred
Prevent
Productive (social function)
Progressive
Protect
Purpose to
Purposive

Reality
Reciprocity
Releasing (capacities)
Rehabilitative
Respect
Responsibility
Restorative
Right

Safeguard
Satisfy (human desires)
Satisfactory (social functioning)

Self-determination
Security
Self-directing
Self-involvement
Self-maximation
Self-realization (of potentials)
Should
Skillful
Spiritual
Standard
Stimulate to
Stimulation
Strengthen
Strengths
Strive to

Suitable
Supply

Togetherness
Trying to

Ultimate
Usefulness (social)

Validity

Welfare
Well-adjusted
Well-being
Wholeness
Worth

WORDS REPRESENTING DISVALUES

Aggressive
Anti-social

Blame
Blaming

Condemnatory
Conflict
Conformity (senseless)
Criminal

Deny (rights)
Destructive
Deterioration
Deviant
Disapprove (behavior)
Disease
Distorted (values)
Dogmatic
Dominate

Harmful
Hate

Ignorance
Indifference
Inequalities
Infringe (on rights of others)
Injustice
Intolerant

Judgment
Judgmental

Limitations

Manipulate
Moralistic
Moralize

Poverty

Self-defeating
Suffering

Uncooperative
Undemocratic

Worse
Wrong

Classified Bibliography

(Numbers Refer to Selected Bibliography, pp. 147–164)

VALUE COMPONENT IN PERSONALITY FORMATION AND SOCIAL WORK PROCESS

AASW,	6	Goldsmith,	88	Parsons, *et al.*,	193
Ackerman,	3	Hallowell,	99	Perlman,	195
Alston,	5	Hamilton,	103	Pettiss,	198
Babcock,	10	Hogan,	110	Phillips,	199
Beck,	16	Hollis,	111	Reid, J. R.,	205
Biestek,	20	Honigmann,	112	Reid, J. H.,	206
———,	21	———,	113	"Relationships," etc.,	208
———,	22	Hutner,	117	Rhode,	210
Bisno,	23	Johnson,	121	Rubins,	219
Cohen,	49	Kahn,	124	Sargent,	221
Cooke, Morris,	52	Kardiner,	128	Smyth,	232
Cooke, Terrence,	53	Kluckhohn, C.,	131	Snelling,	233
Dodson,	69	———,	132	Spencer, K.,	235
———,	70	———,	133	Stein,	238
Eaton & Grover,	72	Kluckhohn, F.,	134	Studt,	242
Fibush,	81	Kozier,	140	Sullivan, D.,	244
Focus, etc.,	83	Krug,	141	Tolman,	250
Furman,	84	Lee,	145	Vasey,	258
Gaynor,	85	MacIver,	163	Williams,	265
Ginsburg,	86	Padula,	190	Witmer,	269
———,	87				

SEMANTICS AND COMMUNICATION PROBLEMS

Benne & Swanson,	18	Feigl,	80	Pratt,	201
Bidney,	19	Ginsburg,	87	Rice,	212
Boulding,	30	Kluckhohn, C.,	132	Roberts,	213
Bower,	31	Lepley,	146	Robertson,	214
(pp. 4, 28, 29)		Lewis,	149	Shaw,	224
Bryson, *et al.*,	35	———,	147	Simpson,	228
———,	36	Meldon,	173	Stevenson,	240
Cooke, Morris,	52	Morris,	182	White, R.,	263
Cumming,	61	Perry,	196	Williams,	264
Davis,	63	———,	197		

SCIENTIFIC METHOD AND VALUES

Benne,	17	Churchman,	43	Palter,	191
———,	18	Edel,	75	Reiser,	207
Boulding,	30	Hartman,	106	Rose,	215
Cattell,	41	Lundberg,	154	Roshwald,	216
———,	42	Lynd,	157	Scheffler,	222
				"Values," etc.,	257

DESCRIPTION OF SOCIAL WORK VALUES AND ETHICS

AASW,	7	Hailman,	96	McCormick,	170
———,	8	Hall,	98	McKenney,	172
Barry,	12	Hamilton,	100	Miller,	178
———,	13	———,	101	Moore,	181
Bisno,	23	———,	103	Murphy,	183
Boehm,	28	Harrison,	105	NASW,	77
Bowers,	32	Herzstein,	107	———,	188
———,	33	Hoey,	109	National Conf.,	14
———,	34	Hollis,	111	Padula,	190
Cannon,	37	Howard,	114	Perlman,	195
———,	38	Hunt,	115	Pray,	202
Cockerill,	44	Jones,	122	Ross,	217
———,	45	Kahn,	125	Roy,	218
Cohen,	50	Kaiser,	126	Russell Sage Fdn.,	78
CSWE,	54	Keith-Lucas,	129	Sheibley,	225
Coyle,	56	Klein,	130	Shur & Shutters,	226
———,	60	Konopka,	138	Smith,	230
de Jongh,	65	———,	139	Sullivan,	64
———,	66	Lindeman,	151	Swift,	247
Eaton & Grover	72	———,	152	The Compass,	249
Eaton,	73	Lindesmith,	153	Towle,	252
———,	74	Lutz,	156	Towley,	254
Eliot,	76	Marcus,	165	Wilson,	266
Govenlock,	89	Marcus,	166	———,	267
Granger,	90	Mayo,	167	Youngdahl,	272
Greenwood,	92	———,	169		

HOW VALUES ARE LEARNED: EDUCATIONAL TECHNIQUES AND PROBLEMS

Allen,	4	Dybwad,	71	Meyer,	177
Barkan & Mooney,	11	Faith,	79	Mooney,	179
Beatman,	15	Grossbard,	93	Parsons,	192
Benne,	17	Handy,	104	Reynolds,	209
Bower,	31	Kadushin,	123	Schweitzer,	223
Counts,	55	Lewin,	148	Sorenson & Dimock,	234
				Towle,	253

EDUCATIONAL CONTENT IN SOCIAL WORK RELATED TO VALUES
AND ETHICS

Abrahamson,	2	Hurlbutt,	116	NASW,	186
Cohen,	48	Hyde & Murphy,	118	———,	187
Coyle,	58	Johnson,	120	———,	188
———,	59	Kadushin,	123	Regensburg,	204
deSchweinitz,	67	Kluckhohn, F.,	134	Smith, E.,	229
Grossbard,	93	McCaffrey,	161	Towle,	253
Hamilton,	102	CSWE,	164	Wessel,	261
Hunt,	115	Moore,	181		

Selected Bibliography

1 Abbott, Edith. *Social Welfare and Professional Education* (Rev. ed.). Chicago: University of Chicago Press, 1942.

2 Abrahamson, Arthur C. "Formulating a Basic Methods Course," *The Social Worker*, XXV, 1 (October, 1956), 3–8.

3 Ackerman, Nathan W. "Mental Hygiene and Social Work, Today and Tomorrow," *Social Casework*, XXXVI, 2 (February, 1955), 63–73.

4 Allen, Jane. "A Student Comments on First Semester Learning," *Social Casework*, XXXVI, 2 (February, 1955), 70–73.

5 Alston, Estelle. "The Leader's Use of Self," in *Readings in Group Work*, ed. Dorothea Sullivan. New York: Association Press, 1952, 25–38.

6 American Association of Schools of Social Work. *Towards an Integrated Program of Professional Education for Social Work: Summary and Findings of Four Workshops*. Annual Meeting, American Association of Schools of Social Work, 1952. (New York: American Association of Schools of Social Work, 1952.)

7 American Association of Social Workers. "Procedures for Considering Complaints of Unethical Conduct of Members." (Approved by the 1953 Delegate Assembly). New York: American Association of Social Workers, No. 2749, 1953.

8 ———. *Standards for the Professional Practice of Social Work*. Supplement to July 1952 *Social Work Journal*, Part II. New York: American Association of Social Workers, 1952.

9 Axtelle, George E. "Philosophy in American Education," *Education Synopsis*. [Publication of New York University, School of Education], December, 1957.

10 Babcock, Charlotte. "The Social Worker in a World of Stress," *Social Service Review*, XXV, 1 (March, 1951), 1–13.

11 Barkan, Manuel and Mooney, Ross L. *Conference on Creativity: A Report to the Rockefeller Foundation*. Columbus: Ohio State University, 1953.

12 Barry, Mildred C. "Community Organization Process," *Social Work Journal*, XXXI, 4 (October, 1950), 157–163.

13 ———. "Current Concepts in Community Organization," in *Group Work and Community Organization, 1956*. New York: National

Conference of Social Work by Columbia University Press, 1956, 1–20.

14 "Basic Problems and Issues," *The Conference Bulletin,* LVIII, 4 (Summer, 1955).

15 Beatman, Francis Levinson. "How Do Professional Workers Become Professional?" in *Casework Papers, 1956,* from the National Conference of Social Work. New York: Family Service Association of America, 1956, 27–36.

16 Beck, Bertram. "The Exile of Those in Conflict with the Law," in *Casework Papers, 1955,* from the National Conference of Social Work. New York: Family Service Association of America, 1955, 32–42.

17 Benne, Kenneth D. "Democratic Ethics in Social Engineering," *Progressive Education,* XXVI (1948–49), 201–207.

18 ———— and Swanson, G. E. "The Problem of Values and the Social Scientist," *Journal of Social Issues,* VI, 4 (1950), 2–7.

19 Bidney, David. "The Concept of Value in Modern Anthropology," in *Anthropology Today,* ed. A. L. Kroeber, *et al.* Chicago: University of Chicago Press, 1953.

20 Biestek, Felix P., S.J. "The Non-Judgmental Attitude," *Social Casework,* XXXIV, 6 (June, 1953), 235–239.

21 ————. *The Principle of Client Self-Determination in Social Casework.* Washington, D.C.: The Catholic University of America Press, 1951.

22 ————. "Religion and Social Casework," in *The Social Welfare Forum, 1956.* New York: National Conference of Social Work by Columbia University Press, 1956, 86–95.

23 Bisno, Herbert. "How Social Will Social Work Be?" *Social Work,* I, 2 (April, 1956), 12–18.

24 ————. *The Philosophy of Social Work.* Washington, D.C.: The Public Affairs Press, 1952.

25 Bixler, Ray and Seeman, Julius. "Suggestions for a Code of Ethics for Consulting Psychologists," *Journal of Abnormal Psychology,* XLI (October, 1946), 486–490.

26 Blacker, Charles. *Human Values in Psychological Medicine.* London: Oxford University Press, 1933.

27 Blauch, Lloyd E. (ed.). *Education for the Professions.* Washington, D.C.: United States Department of Health, Education, and Welfare, 1955.

28 Boehm, Werner W. "The Role of Values in Social Work," *The Jewish Social Service Quarterly,* XXVI, 4 (June, 1950), 429–438.

29 Boehm, Werner W. "Social Work and the Social Sciences," *Journal of Psychiatric Social Work,* XXI, 1 (September, 1951), 4–8.

30 Boulding, K. E. "Some Contributions of Economics to the General Theory of Value," *Philosophy of Science,* XXIII, 1 (January, 1956), 1–14.

31 Bower, William Clayton. *Moral and Spiritual Values in Education.* Lexington: University of Kentucky Press, 1952.

32 Bowers, Swithun, O.M.I. "Human Values and Public Welfare,"*The Social Worker,* XXIII (December, 1954), 1–7.

33 ——. "Social Work and Human Problems," *Social Casework,* XXXV, 5 (May, 1954), 187–192.

34 ——. "Some Reflections on Being a Member of a Profession," *The Social Worker,* XXIV, 1 (October, 1956), 1–6.

35 Bryson, Lyman and Finkelstein, Louis (eds.). *Science, Philosophy and Religion.* Third Symposium [on Meaning of Values]. New York: Conference on Science and Religion, 1943, Editorial Introduction, 3–7.

36 Bryson, Lyman, *et al. Symbols and Values.* New York: Conference on Science and Religion by Harper & Brothers, 1954.

37 Cannon, Mary Antoinette. "Guiding Motives in Social Work," in *New Directions in Social Work,* ed. Cora Kasius. New York: Harper & Brothers, 1954, 13–30.

38 ——. "Underlying Principles and Common Practices in Social Work," in *Readings in Social Case Work,* ed. Fern Lowry. New York: Columbia University Press, 1939, 14–21.

39 Carr-Saunders, A. M. and Wilson, P. A. *The Professions.* Oxford: The Clarendon Press, 1933.

40 ——. "Profession," *Encyclopaedia of the Social Sciences,* XII, 476–480.

41 Cattell, Raymond B. "Ethics and the Social Sciences," *The American Psychologist,* III (June, 1948), 193–198.

42 ——. "The Integration of Psychology with Moral Values," *The British Journal of Psychology,* XLI (September, 1950), 25–33.

43 Churchman, C. West. "Sciences and Decision Making," *Philosophy of Science,* XXIII, 3 (July, 1956), 247–249.

44 Cockerill, Eleanor E., *et al. A Conceptual Framework for Social Casework* (2nd ed.). Pittsburgh: University of Pittsburgh Press, 1953.

45 Cockerill, Eleanor E. "The Interdependence of the Professions in Helping People," in *The Social Welfare Forum, 1953.* New York: The National Conference of Social Work by Columbia University Press, 1953, 137–147.

46　"Code of the Chest and Council Movement," *Community* (April, 1953), 16ff.

47　Cogan, Morris L. "Toward a Definition of Profession," *The Harvard Educational Review,* XXIII, 1 (Winter, 1953), 33–50.

48　Cohen, Nathan E. "Desegregation—A Challenge to the Place of Moral Values in Social Work Education," *Proceedings* of Third Annual Program Meeting of the Council on Social Work Education, 1955. New York: Council on Social Work Education, 1955.

49　————. "The Place of the Sectarian Agency in Services to Groups," in *The Social Welfare Forum, 1951.* New York: National Conference of Social Work by Columbia University Press, 1951, 271–280.

50　————. "Professional Social Work Faces the Future," *Social Work Journal,* XXXVI, 3 (July, 1955), 79–86.

51　"The Content of Family Social Work," (Family Service Association of America Committee Report), *Social Casework,* XXXVII, 7 (July, 1956), 319–326.

52　Cooke, Morris Llwellyn. "Professional Ethics and Social Change," *The American Scholar,* XV, 487–497.

53　Cooke, Terence J. "The Group Members and the Group Work Process in the Light of Thomistic Philosophy," in *Readings in Group Work,* ed. Dorothea Sullivan. New York: Association Press, 1952, 160–178.

54　Council on Social Work Education. *Social Work as a Profession.* New York: Council on Social Work Education, 1953.

55　Counts, George S. *Education and American Civilization.* New York: Bureau of Publications, Teachers College, Columbia University Press, 1952.

56　Coyle, Grace L. *Group Experience and Democratic Values.* New York: Woman's Press, 1947.

57　————. "New Insights Available to the Social Worker from the Social Sciences," *Social Service Review,* XXVI, 3 (September, 1952), 289–304.

58　————. "The Objectives and Structure of the New Curriculum," *Proceedings* of the Third Annual Program Meeting of the Council on Social Work Education, 1955. New York: Council on Social Work Education, 1955.

59　————. "The Role of Teacher in the Creation of an Integrated Curriculum," *Social Work Journal,* XXXIII, 2 (April, 1952), 73–82.

60　————. "The Social Worker and His Society," *Social Service Review,* XXX, 4 (December, 1956), 387–399.

61   Cumming, John and Elaine. "Affective Symbolism, Social Norms, and Mental Illness," *Psychiatry*, XIX, 1 (February, 1956), 77–85.

62   Cunningham, Ruth and Associates. "Group Discipline," in *Readings in Group Work*, ed. Dorothea Sullivan. New York: Association Press, 1952, 72–77.

63   Davis, Kingsley. *Human Society*. New York: Macmillan Co., 1949.

64   "Definition of Group Work," in *Readings in Social Group Work*, ed. Dorothea Sullivan. New York: Association Press, 1952, Appendix, 420.

65   deJongh, J. F. "Man's Quest for Freedom and Security: Implications for Social Work Education in the Twentieth Century." [Presented in the Graduate School of Social Work Seminar, University of Pittsburgh, May 10, 1957.] (Mimeographed.) "Comments" by Eveline Burns. (Typewritten.)

66   ———. "Self-Help in Modern Society," *Social Work Journal*, XXXV, 4 (October, 1954), 139–144; 166–168.

67   deSchweinitz, Karl. "Social Values and Social Action—the Intellectual Base as Illustrated in the Study of History," *Social Service Review*, XXX, 2 (June, 1956), 119–131.

68   Dewey, John. "Philosophy," *Encyclopaedia of the Social Sciences*, XII. New York: The Macmillan Company, 1934. 118–128.

69   Dodson, Dan W. "Human Relations and Post War Metropolitan Growth," Address to B'nai B'rith Youth Organization, Washington, D.C., 1957. (Mimeographed.)

70   ———. "Moral and Ethical Values." [Notes on speech given in Workshop on Moral and Ethical Values, Committee on Youth Services, National Social Welfare Assembly, June 6, 1957.]

71   Dybwad, Gunnar and Goller, Gertrude. "Goals and Techniques of Parent Education," in *Casework Papers, 1955*, from the National Conference of Social Work. New York: Family Service Association of America, 1955, 137–148.

72   Eaton, Arthur and Grover, Elizabeth. "Ethical and Value Considerations in Social Group Work Within the Framework of a Democratic Society." (Mimeographed, Doctoral Seminar in Social Group Work, New York School of Social Work, Columbia University, 1956.)

73   Eaton, Joseph W. "How Values Affect Social Practice." (Typewritten.)

74   ———. "Whence and Whither Social Work?" *Social Work*, I, 1 (January, 1956), 11–26.

75   Edel, Abraham. *Ethical Judgment: The Use of Science in Ethics*. New York: Free Press, 1955.

76   Eliot, Martha. "The Family Today: Its Needs and Opportunities," *Social Casework*, XXXIV, 2 (February, 1953), 47–54.

77   "Ethical Issues in Social Work," *Social Work Journal*, XXXVI, 2 (April, 1955), 46.

78   "Experimental Draft of a Code of Ethics for Social Case Workers." [Authorship attributed to Mary E. Richmond. Printed but not published, ca. 1924.] New York: Charity Organization Department, Russell Sage Foundation, now in Charity Organization Department Files, Archives, Library of the New York School of Social Work, Columbia University.

79   Faith, Goldie Basch. "The Professional School and the Social Agency," in *Professional Education Based in Practice*. Philadelphia: School of Social Work, University of Pennsylvania, 1953.

80   Feigl, Herbert. "An Analysis of the Nature and the Limits of Ethical Arguments." (Mimeographed.)

81   Fibush, Esther. "The Evaluation of Marital Interaction in the Treatment of One Partner," *Social Casework*, XXXVIII, 6 (June, 1957), 303–307.

82   Fisk, Rev. D. M. "Suggested Readings in Social Ethics," in "Sociological Reading References," *Chicago Commons*, I, 1 (April, 1896), 10.

83   "Focus on the Multi-Problem Family," *Youth Board News*, May, 1957, 3.

84   Furman, Sylvan S. (ed.) *Reaching the Unreached* (2nd ed.) . New York: New York City Youth Board, 1954.

85   Gaynor, Elizabeth. "Religion as a Resource in the Adjustment of Catholic Patients Following Hospitalization for a Mental Illness." Unpublished Master's project. New York School of Social Work, Columbia University, 1949.

86   Ginsburg, Sol Wiener. "The Impact of the Social Worker's Cultural Structure on Social Therapy," *Social Casework*, XXXII, 8 (October, 1951), 319–325.

87   ———. "Values and the Psychiatrist," *American Journal of Orthopsychiatry*, XX, 3 (July, 1950), 466–478.

88   Goldsmith, Jane K. "The Unmarried Mother's Search for Standards," *Social Casework*, XXXVIII, 2 (February, 1957), 69–74.

89   Govenlock, Shaun. "Professional Social Work, Its Basic Assumptions," *The Social Worker*, XXV, 2 (January, 1957), 4–9.

90   Granger, Lester B. "Basic Human Needs," Social Work Journal, XXXIV, 2 (April, 1953), 67–70; 87ff.

91   ———. "Social Work's Response to Democracy's Challenge," in *The*

Social Welfare Forum, 1952. New York: The National Conference of Social Work by Columbia University Press, 1952.

92 Greenwood, Ernest. "Attributes of a Profession," *Social Work,* II, 3 (July, 1957), 45–55.

93 Grossbard, Hyman. "Methodology for Developing Self-Awareness," *Social Casework,* XXXV, 9 (November, 1954), 380–386.

94 *A Guide to Classification of Professional Positions and Evaluation Outlines in a Family Service Agency.* New York: Family Service Association of America, 1957.

95 Hackbusch, Florence. "Professional Ethics in Institution Practice," *The American Psychologist,* III (March, 1948), 85–87.

96 Hailman, David E. "A Code of Ethics for Social Workers," *Social Work Journal,* XXX, 2 (April, 1949), 44–50.

97 Hall, Everett W. *Modern Science and Human Values: A Study in the History of Ideas.* Princeton, N.J.: D. Van Nostrand Co., Inc., 1956.

98 Hall, L. K. "Group Workers and Professional Ethics," *The Group,* XV, 1 (October, 1952), 3–8.

99 Hallowell, A. Irving. "Values, Acculturation and Mental Health," *American Journal of Orthopsychiatry,* XX, 4 (October, 1950), 732–743.

100 Hamilton, Gordon. "Helping People—The Growth of a Profession," in *Social Work As Human Relations.* New York: Columbia University Press, 1949, 3–18.

101 ———. "The Role of Social Casework in Social Policy," *Social Casework,* XXXIII, 8 (October, 1952), 316–324.

102 ———. "Self-Awareness in Professional Education," *Social Casework,* XXXV, 9 (November, 1954), 371–379.

103 ———. *Theory and Practice of Social Case Work* (2nd ed. rev.). New York: Columbia University Press, 1951.

104 Handy, Rollo. "Personality Factors and Intellectual Production," *Philosophy of Science,* XXIII, 4 (October, 1956), 325–332.

105 Harrison, Ethel. "From Malthus to Marcus." Unpublished manuscript, University of Minnesota, 1954.

106 Hartman, George W. "Value as the Unifying Concept of the Social Sciences," *Journal of Social Psychology,* X, 4 (November, 1939), 563–575.

107 Herzstein, Elsbeth. "The Goals of Social Work and Public Education." Unpublished Master's project, New York School of Social Work, Columbia University, 1948.

108 Hobbs, Nicholas. "The Development of a Code of Ethical Standards

for Psychology," *The American Psychologist,* III (March, 1948), 80–84.

109 Hoey, Jane M. "Human Rights and Social Work," in *Social Work in the Current Scene.* New York: The National Conference of Social Work by Columbia University Press, 1950.

110 Hogan, Margaret. "Psychiatric Social Work in Mental Hospitals," in *Education for Psychiatric Social Work,* Proceedings of the Dartmouth Conference. The National Institute for Mental Health, 1949.

111 Hollis, Florence. "The Generic and Specific in Social Casework Reexamined," *Social Casework,* XXXVII, 5 (May, 1956), 211–219.

112 Honigmann, John J. *Culture and Personality.* New York: Harper & Brothers, 1954.

113 ———. "Toward a Distinction Between Psychiatric and Social Abnormality," *Social Forces,* XXXI, 3 (March, 1953), 274–277.

114 Howard, Donald S. "The Common Core of Social Work in Different Countries," *Social Work Journal,* XXXII, 4 (October, 1951), 163–171.

115 Hunt, Margery Kohl. "Integrating the Non-Judgmental Attitude with Social Responsibility and Authority in Social Casework." Unpublished Master's thesis, School of Social Work, University of Connecticut, 1957.

116 Hurlbutt, Mary. "Cultural Factors in Practice and Training," *Jewish Social Service Quarterly,* XXVI, 3 (March, 1950), 309–315.

117 Hutner, Florence. "Professional Responsibility and Leadership Development," *Jewish Social Service Quarterly,* XXX, 3 (Spring, 1954), 239–241.

118 Hyde, Alice B. and Murphy, Jeane. "An Experiment in Integrative Learning," *Social Service Review,* XXIX, 4 (December, 1955), 358–371.

119 Jahoda, Marie, *et al. Research Methods in Social Relations.* New York: The Dryden Press, 1951, Part I.

120 Johnson, Arlien. "Educating Professional Social Workers for Ethical Practice," *Social Service Review,* XXIX, 2 (June, 1955), 125–136.

121 Johnson, F. Ernest (ed.). *Religion and Social Work.* (Religion and Civilization Series.) New York: The Institute for Religious and Social Studies, Harper & Brothers, Distributors, 1956.

122 Jones, Hubert Eugene. "An Exploratory Study of Social Work Values in Relation to Social Work Practice." Unpublished Master's essay, School of Social Work, Boston University, 1957.

123   Kadushin, Alfred. "Interview Observations as a Teaching Device," *Social Casework,* XXXVII, 7 (July, 1956), 334–341.

124   Kahn, Alfred J. "First Principles in Planning Community Service to Deal with Children in Trouble," *Social Service Review,* XXX, 4 (December, 1956), 415–427.

125   ———. "The Nature of Social Work Knowledge," in *New Directions in Social Work,* ed. Cora Kasius. New York: Harper & Brothers, 1954.

126   Kaiser, Clara. "Social Group Work Practice and Social Resposibility," in *The Social Welfare Forum, 1952.* New York: National Conference of Social Work by Columbia University Press, 1952.

127   Kallen, Horace M. "Morals," *Encyclopaedia of the Social Sciences,* X. New York: The Macmillan Company, 1934. 643–647.

128   Kardiner, Abram. *The Individual and His Society.* New York: Columbia University Press, 1939.

129   Keith-Lucas, Alan. "The Political Theory Implied in Social Casework Theory," *American Political Science Review,* XLVII (December, 1953), 1076ff.

130   Klein, Alan F. *Society, Democracy and the Group.* New York: Woman's Press and William Morrow & Co., 1953.

131   Kluckhohn, Clyde. *Mirror for Man.* New York: Whittlesey House, 1949.

132   ———. "Values and Value Orientation in the Theory of Action," in *Toward a General Theory of Action,* ed. Talcott Parsons and Edward A. Shils. Cambridge, Mass.: Harvard University Press, 1951, 388–433.

133   ——— and Murray, Henry A. (eds.). "Personality Formation: The Determinants," *Personality in Nature, Society, and Culture* (2nd ed., rev. & enlarged; New York: Alfred A. Knopf, 1953), 53–67.

134   Kluckhohn, Florence Rockwood. "Cultural Factors in Social Work Practice and Education," *Social Service Review,* XXV, 1 (March, 1951), 38–47.

135   ———. "Dominant and Variant Value Orientations," in *Personality in Nature, Society, and Culture,* ed. Clyde Kluckhohn and Henry A. Murray (2nd ed. rev.). New York: Alfred A. Knopf, 1953, 342–357.

136   Kohn, Robert D. "Introductory Remarks," in *The Future of the Professions in America.* Proceedings of the Second Institute on Human Relations of the New York Society for Ethical Culture, n. d.

137   ———. "The Significance of the Professional Ideal: Professional Ethics and the Public Interest," *The Annals,* CI (May, 1922), 1–5.

138   Konopka, Gisela. "The Generic and Specific in Group Work Practice

in the Psychiatric Setting," *Social Work,* I, 1 (January, 1956), 72–80.

139 Konopka, Gisela. "Social Work's Search for a Philosophy with Special Reference to Eduard C. Lindeman." Unpublished doctor's dissertation, The New York School of Social Work, Columbia University, 1957. [To be published by Minnesota Press, 1958.]

140 Kozier, Ada. "Casework with Parents of Children Born with Severe Brain Defects," *Social Casework,* XXXVIII, 4 (April, 1957), 183–189.

141 Krug, Othilda. "The Dynamic Use of the Ego Function in Casework Practice," *Social Casework,* XXXVI, 10 (December, 1955), 443–450.

142 Krughoff, Merrill F. "Review of Community Organization Practice," by Campbell G. Murphy, *Social Work Journal,* XXXV, 4 (October, 1954), 178–179.

143 Landis, Benson Y. (ed.). "Ethical Standards and Professional Conduct," (a symposium), *The Annals of the American Academy of Political and Social Science,* 297 (January, 1955), 1–124.

144 ———. *Professional Codes.* New York: Teachers College, Columbia University, 1927.

145 Lee, Dorothy. "Are Basic Needs Ultimate?" in *Personality in Nature, Society, and Culture,* ed. Clyde Kluckhohn and Henry A. Murray (2nd ed. rev.). New York: Alfred A. Knopf, 1953, 335–341.

146 Lepley, Ray. *The Language of Value.* New York: Columbia University Press, 1957.

147 ———. (ed.). *Value, A Cooperative Inquiry.* New York: Columbia University Press, 1949.

148 Lewin, Kurt. "Conduct, Knowledge, and Acceptance of New Values," in *Resolving Social Conflicts,* ed. Gertrude W. Lewin. New York: Harper & Brothers, 1948, 56–68.

149 Lewis, Clarence Irving. *The Ground and Nature of the Right.* New York: Columbia University Press, 1955.

150 Lewis, Ray and Maude, Angus. *Professional People.* London: Phoenix House, Ltd., 1952.

151 Lindeman, Eduard C. "Democracy and Social Work," in *Proceedings of the National Conference of Social Work, 1948.* New York: National Conference of Social Work by Columbia University Press, 1948, 79–88.

152 ———. "The Roots of Democratic Culture," in *Group Work Foundations and Frontiers,* ed. Harleigh B. Trecker. New York: Whiteside, Inc., 1955, 13–25.

153 Lindesmith, Alfred R. and Strauss, Anselm L. "Critique of Culture-

Personality Writings," *American Sociological Review,* XV, 5 (October, 1950), 587–600.

154 Lundberg, George A. "Can Science Validate Ethics?" *Bulletin of the American Association of University Professors,* XXXVI (1950), 261–275.

155 Lurie, Harry L. "The Responsibilities of a Socially Oriented Profession," in *New Directions in Social Work,* ed. Cora Kasius. New York: Harper & Brothers, 1954, 31–53.

156 Lutz, Werner A. *Concepts and Principles Underlying Social Casework Practice.* Washington, D.C.: National Association of Social Workers, Medical Social Work Section, 1956.

157 Lynd, Robert. *Knowledge for What?* Princeton: Princeton University Press, 1939.

158 Mannheim, Karl. *Essays on the Sociology of Knowledge,* ed. Paul Kecskemeti. New York: Oxford University Press, 1952.

159 ———. *Men and Society in an Age of Reconstruction.* Translated by Edward A. Shils. New York: Harcourt Brace & Co., 1940.

160 Maritain, Jacques (ed.) *Human Rights, Comments and Interpretations.* (A symposium sponsored by the United Nations Educational, Scientific and Cultural Organization.) New York: Columbia University Press, 1949.

161 McCaffery, Miriam. "Criteria for Student Progress in Field Work," *Journal of Social Casework,* XXVIII, 1 (January, 1947), 9–17.

162 MacIver, Robert M. (ed.). *Conflict of Loyalties.* New York: The Institute for Religious and Social Studies, Harper & Brothers, Distributors, 1952.

163 ———. *The Pursuit of Happiness.* New York: Simon & Schuster, Inc., 1955.

164 *Manual of Accrediting Standards for Graduate Schools of Social Work.* New York: Council on Social Work Education. (Revised as of May 1, 1957.)

165 Marcus, Grace F. "The Advance of Social Casework in Its Distinct Social Usefulness," *Social Casework,* XXXVI, 9 (November, 1955), 391–399.

166 ———. "Helping the Client to Use His Capacities and Resources," *Proceedings of the National Conference of Social Work, 1948.* New York: Columbia University Press, 1949, 251–259.

167 Mayo, Leonard W. "Basic Issues in Social Work," *Proceedings of the National Conference of Social Work, 1948.* New York: Columbia University Press, 1949, 12–30.

168 Mayo, Leonard W. "Putting Our Present Knowledge to Work," *Social Work Journal*, XXXII, 1 (January, 1951), 4ff.

169 ———. "Spiritual Factors in Social Work," in *Religion and Social Work*, ed. F. Ernest Johnson. New York: Harper & Brothers, 1956, 71–81.

170 McCormick, Mary J. *Diagnostic Casework in the Thomistic Pattern.* New York: Columbia University Press, 1954.

171 McGreal, Ian. *The Art of Making Choices.* Dallas: Southern Methodist Press, 1953.

172 McKenney, Charles R. *Moral Problems in Social Work.* Milwaukee: Bruce Publishing Co., 1951.

173 Meldon, A. E. *Ethical Theories.* New York: Prentice Hall, 1955.

174 Merton, Robert K. "Bureaucratic Structure and Personality," in *Studies in Leadership*, ed. Alvin Goulder. New York: Harper & Brothers, 1950, 67ff.

175 ——— and Kitt, Alice S. "Contributions to the Theory of Reference Group Behavior," in *Continuities in Social Research*, ed. Robert K. Merton and Paul F. Lazarsfeld. Glencoe, Ill.: The Free Press, 1950, 40–105.

176 Messner, Johannes. *Social Ethics: Natural Law in the Modern World.* Translated by J. J. Doherty. St. Louis: B. Herder Book Co., 1949.

177 Meyer, Agnes E. *Education for a New Morality.* New York: The Macmillan Co., 1957.

178 Miller, Irving. "A Critical Appraisal of Some Aspects of Social Group Work Theory and Practice," in *Group Work and Community Organization, 1955.* New York: The National Conference of Social Work by Columbia University Press, 1955, 66–77.

179 Mooney, Ross L. "Cultural Blocks and Creative Possibilities," *Educational Leadership*, XIII (February, 1956), 273–278.

180 ———. "Evaluating Graduate Education," *Harvard Educational Review*, XXV (Spring, 1955), 85–94.

181 Moore, John O. "The Task of Social Work Education Today and Tomorrow," *The Social Worker*, XXIII, 4 (April, 1955), 10–20.

182 Morris, Charles. *Varieties of Human Value.* Chicago: University of Chicago Press, 1956.

183 Murphy, Campbell G. *Community Organization Practice.* Cambridge, Mass.: The Riverside Press, 1954.

184 Myrdal, Gunnar. *An American Dilemma.* New York: Harper & Brothers, 1944. Appendix 1, "Note on Valuation and Beliefs," 1027–1034. Appendix 2, "A Methodological Note on Facts and Valuations in Social Science," 1035–1070.

185 National Association of Social Workers. Delegate Assembly *Workbook I*, Delegate Assembly *Workbook II*. New York: National Association of Social Workers, 1958.

186 ———. "Goals of Public Social Policy." Unpublished draft, 1956.

187 ———. "Procedures for the Consideration of Complaints Against Agencies for Violations of Social Work Personnel Practices." (Master copy, mimeographed.) New York: National Association of Social Workers, No. 546–23/S.

188 ———. *Standards for Personnel Practices*. New York: National Association of Social Workers, 1957.

189 Oxnam, C. Bromley. "Goals for Social Work in a Contemporary Society," in *Proceedings of the National Conference of Social Work, 1948*. New York: Columbia University Press, 1949, 89–100.

190 Padula, Helen. "Some Thoughts About the Culture of Social Work," *Journal of Psychiatric Social Work*, XXIII, 4 (April, 1954), 172–176.

191 Palter, Robert. "Philosophic Principles and Scientific Theory," *Philosophy of Science*, XXIII, 2 (April, 1956), 111–135.

192 Parsons, Talcott. *Religious Perspective of College Teaching in Sociology Social Psychology*. New Haven: Edward W. Hogan Foundation, 1951.

193 ———, Shils, Edward A. and Olds, James. "Values, Motives, and Systems of Action," in *Toward a General Theory of Action*, ed. T. Parsons and E. A. Shils. Cambridge, Mass.: Harvard University Press, 1951.

194 "The Parting of the Ways," [Editorial] *The Catholic Charities Review*, XL, 6 (June, 1956), 3–4.

195 Perlman, Helen Harris. *Social Case Work*. Chicago: University of Chicago Press, 1957.

196 Perry, Ralph Barton. *General Theory of Value*. New York: Longmans, Green & Co., 1926.

197 ———. *Realms of Value*. Cambridge, Mass.: Harvard University Press, 1954.

198 Pettiss, Susan. "Casework with Families Separated by National Boundaries," *Social Casework*, XXXVII, 9 (November, 1956), 433–437.

199 Phillips, Helen U. (ed.). *Achievement of Responsible Behavior Through Group Work Process*. Philadelphia: School of Social Work, University of Pennsylvania, 1950.

200 Polansky, Norman *et al.* "Social Workers in Society: Results of a Sampling Study," *Social Work Journal*, XXXIV, 2 (April, 1953), 74–80.

201 Pratt, James B. "The Nature of Value," in *Science, Philosophy and Religion*, ed. Lyman Bryson and Louis Finkelstein. New York: Conference on Science, Philosophy and Religion, 1943.

202 Pray, Kenneth L. M. "Social Work and Social Action," in *Proceedings of the National Conference of Social Work, 1945*. New York: National Conference of Social Work by Columbia University Press, 1945, 350–359.

203 *Proceedings of the Midcentury White House Conference on Children and Youth*, ed. Edward A. Richards. Raleigh, N.C.: Health Publications Institute, 1951, esp. 28–40.

204 Regensburg, Jeanette. "Professional Attributes, Knowledge, and Shills in Practice: Educational Priorities," *Social Work Journal,* XXXIV, 2 (April, 1953), 51–54.

205 Reid, John R. "The Problem of Values in Psychoanalysis," *American Journal of Psychoanalysis,* XV, 2 (1955), 115–122.

206 Reid, Joseph H. "Principles, Values and Assumptions Underlying Adoption Practice," in *The Social Welfare Forum, 1956*. New York: National Conference of Social Work by Columbia University Press, 1956.

207 Reiser, Oliver L. "Postulates for an Ethics of Belief in Science, Religion, and Philosophy," *Philosophy of Science,* XXIII, 4 (October, 1956), 280–282.

208 "The Relationship Between Religion and Psychotherapy in the Adjustment of the Individual" (a symposium), *Journal of Psychiatric Social Work,* XVIII, 1 (Autumn, 1948), 59–80.

209 Reynolds, Bertha Capen. *Learning and Teaching in the Practice of Social Work.* New York: Farrar & Rinehart, Inc., 1942.

210 Rhode, Carl. "Psychiatric Work in the Adult Mental Hygiene Clinic," in *Education for Psychiatric Social Work,* Proceedings of the Dartmouth Conference. The National Institute for Mental Health. New York: American Association of Psychiatric Social Workers, 1950.

211 Rice, Philip B. "Definitions in Value Theory," *The Journal of Philosophy,* XLIV (January, 1947), 57–67.

212 ——. *On the Knowledge of Good and Evil.* New York: Random House, 1955.

213 Roberts, William Henry. *The Problem of Choice.* Boston: Ginn & Co., 1941.

214 Robertson, J. M. *A Short History of Morals.* London: Watts & Co., 1920.

215 Rose, Arnold M. "The Social Responsibility of the Social Scientist," *Social Problems,* I (January, 1954), 85–90.

216 Roshwald, M. "Value-Judgments in the Social Sciences," *The British Journal for the Philosophy of Science,* VI (November, 1955), 186–208.

217 Ross, Murray G. *Community Organization.* New York: Harper & Brothers, 1955.

218 Roy, Agnes. "Code of Ethics," *The Social Worker,* XXIII, 1 (October, 1954), 4–7.

219 Rubins, Jack L. "Neurotic Attitudes Toward Religion," *American Journal of Psychoanalysis,* XV, 1 (1955), 71–81.

220 Sanders, Marion K. "Social Work: A Profession Chasing Its Tail," *Harper's Magazine,* CCXIV (March, 1957), 59ff.

221 Sargent, Helen. "Professional Ethics and Problems of Therapy," *Journal of Abnormal Psychology,* XL (January, 1945), 47–60.

222 Scheffler, Israel. "Civilization and Value: A Review," *Harvard Educational Review,* XXIII, 110ff.

223 Schweitzer, Albert. *Out of My Life and Thought.* Translated by C. T. Campion. (A Mentor Book.) New York: Henry Holt & Co., Inc., 1949.

224 Shaw, Mary J. "Social Valuation," in *Modern American Society,* ed. Kingsley Davis, Harry C. Bredemeier and Marion J. Levy. New York: Rinehart, 1949.

225 Sheibley, G. Evangeline. "Impressions of the International Conference of Social Work," *Social Casework,* XXXVII, 10 (December, 1956), 489–493.

226 Shur, Harriet R. and Shutters, Joyce. "A Study in Attitudes and Values of a Group of Second Year Students at the New York School of Social Work." Unpublished Master's project, New York School of Social Work, Columbia University, 1956.

227 Simmons, Leo W. and Wolff, Harold. *Social Science in Medicine.* New York: Russell Sage Foundation, 1954.

228 Simpson, George. "Some Problems for Social Philosophy," *Bulletin of the American Association of University Professors,* XXXVI (1950), 516–524.

229 Smith, Elliott Dunlap. "Education and the Task of Making Social Work Professional," *Social Service Review,* XXXI, 1 (March, 1957), 1–10.

230 Smith, Sophie Jacob. "*The New York Times* Hundred Neediest Cases: Analysis of the Changes in the Appeals of 1930, 1939, and 1956."

Unpublished Master's project, Graduate School of Public Administration and Social Service, New York University, 1957.

231 Smith, T. V. "Ethics," *Encyclopaedia of the Social Sciences,* V, 602–606.

232 Smyth, Wilma. "The Rural Child Welfare Worker in Action," *Social Casework,* XXXVI, 9 (November, 1955), 406–412.

233 Snelling, Jean M. "Professional Leadership in the Social Structure," *Social Casework,* XXXV, 7 (July, 1954), 279–284.

234 Sorenson, Roy and Dimock, Hedley S. *Designing Education in Values.* New York: Association Press, 1955.

235 Spencer, Katherine. "The Place of Socio-Cultural Study in Casework," in *Socio-Cultural Elements in Casework.* New York: Council on Social Work Education. 1953.

236 Spencer, Sue. "Religion and Social Work," *Social Work,* I, 3 (July 1956), 19–26.

237 Stein, Herman. "Social Science in Social Work Practice and Education," *Social Casework,* XXXVI, 4 (April, 1955), 147–155.

238 ———. "Socio-cultural Factors in Psychiatric Clinics for Children," *Social Service Review,* XXX, 1 (March, 1956), 9–19.

239 Sterecker, Ralph Little. "Moot Questions in Psychiatric Ethics," *American Journal of Psychiatry,* CXIII, 5 (November, 1956), 455–460.

240 Stevenson, Charles Leslie. *Ethics and Language.* New Haven: Yale University Press, 1948.

241 Stewart, Judge V. Lorne. "Family Breakdown," *Canadian Welfare,* June, 1957.

242 Studt, Elliot. "The Contribution of Correctional Practice to Social Work Theory and Education," *Social Casework,* XXXVII, 6 (June, 1956), 263–269.

243 ———. "Value Systems and Juvenile Delinquency," in *Group Work and Community Organization Papers.* New York: National Conference of Social Work by Columbia University Press, 1956, 21–29.

244 Sullivan, Dorothea S. (ed.). *Readings in Social Group Work.* New York: Association Press, 1952.

245 Sullivan, Harry Stack. *The Interpersonal Theory of Psychiatry.* New York: W. W. Norton & Co., Inc., 1953.

246 Sutich, Anthony. "Toward a Professional Code for Psychological Consultants," *Journal of Abnormal Psychology,* XXXIX (July, 1944), 329–350.

247 Swift, Linton B. "A Social Worker's Creed," *Highlights,* IV, 8 (October, 1943).

248 Taeusch, C. F. "Professional Ethics," *Encyclopaedia of the Social Sciences,* XII, 472–476.

249   "Tentative Criteria of Professional Conduct," *The Compass,* XXII
        (August, 1941), 2–4.
250   Tolman, Edward Chase. "Psychological Man," *Journal of Social Psy-
        chology,* XIII (February, 1941), 205–218.
251   Timasheff, Nicholas S. *Sociological Theory: Its Nature and Growth,*
        Garden City, N.Y.: Doubleday & Co., Inc., 1955.
252   Towle, Charlotte. *Common Human Needs.* New York: American Asso-
        ciation of Social Workers, 1953.
253   ———. *The Learner in Education for the Professions.* Chicago: Uni-
        versity of Chicago Press, 1954.
254   Towley, Louis H. "Professional Responsibility in a Democracy," in
        Education for Social Work, Proceedings 1953 Annual Program
        Meeting. New York: Council on Social Work Education, 1953, 10–
        21.
255   Trecker, Harleigh B. (ed.). *Group Work Foundations and Frontiers.*
        New York: Whiteside, Inc., 1955.
256   Tyler, Ralph E. "Educational Problems in Other Professions," in *Edu-
        cation for Librarianship,* ed. Bernard Berelson. Chicago: Amer-
        ican Library Association, 1949.
257   "Values and the Social Scientist" (a symposium), ed. Kenneth D. Benne
        and C. E. Swanson, *Journal of Social Issues,* VI, 4 (1950).
258   Vasey, Wayne. "Public Relations, An Inescapable Obligation in Social
        Welfare," *Social Service Review,* XXVII, 4 (December, 1953), 394–
        398.
259   "Violations of Personnel Practices in Social Work: Report for July
        1952–June 1954," *Social Work Journal,* XXXV, 4 (October, 1954),
        138ff.
260   Warach, Bernard. "Social Group Work and Sectarian Purpose." Un-
        published mimeographed manuscript, Doctoral Seminar in Social
        Group Work, New York School of Social Work, Columbia Uni-
        versity, 1955.
261   Wessel, Rosa. "The Place of Practice in Education for Social Work,"
        in *Professional Education Based in Practice.* Philadelphia: School
        of Social Work, University of Pennsylvania, 1953.
262   White, Morton G. *Social Thought in America.* New York: Viking Press,
        Inc., 1949.
263   White, Ralph K. *Value Analysis.* New York: Society for the Psycho-
        logical Study of Social Issues, 1951.
264   Williams, Robin M., Jr. *American Society.* New York: Alfred A. Knopf,
        1951.

265   Williams, Robin M., Jr. "Religion, Value Orientations, and Intergroup Conflict," *Journal of Social Issues,* XII, 3 (1956), 12–20.

266   Wilson, Gertrude. "Social Group Work: Trends and Developments," *Social Work,* I, 4 (October, 1956), 66–75.

267   ———, and Ryland, Gladys. *Social Group Work Practice.* Boston: Houghton, Mifflin Co., 1949.

268   Winston, Ellen. "Sounder Public Welfare Programs Through Adequate Staffing," *Public Welfare News* (North Carolina State Department of Public Welfare), XX, 1 (March, 1957), 1–6.

269   Witmer, Helen. "Juvenile Delinquency and Anomie," *Children,* II, 5 (September–October, 1955), 188–191.

270   Woods, Sister Frances Jerome. *Cultural Values of American Ethnic Groups.* New York: Harper & Brothers, 1956.

271   Young, Donald. "Sociology and the Practicing Professions," *American Sociological Review,* XX (December, 1955), 641–648.

272   Youngdahl, Benjamin E. "What We Believe," in *The Social Welfare Forum, 1952.* New York: National Conference of Social Work by Columbia University Press, 1952, 29–45.

HETERICK MEMORIAL LIBRARY
361.301 P983t   onuu
Pumphrey, Muriel Wa/The teaching of valu

3 5111 00126 8253